Create
Your Own
Dreams

Create Your Own Dreams

A Seth Workbook

Nancy Ashley

PRENTICE
HALL
PRESS

New York   London   Toronto   Sydney   Tokyo   Singapore

Unknown Reality: Volume I by Jane Roberts. Copyright © 1977. Reprinted by permission of Prentice-Hall, Inc.

The Nature of the Psyche by Jane Roberts. Copyright © 1979. Reprinted by permission of Prentice-Hall, Inc.

Conversations with Seth: Volume II by Susan M. Watkins. Copyright © 1981. Reprinted by permission of Prentice-Hall, Inc.

Prentice Hall Press
15 Columbus Circle
New York, NY 10023

Library of Congress Cataloging-in-Publication Data

Ashley, Nancy.
    Create your own dreams : a Seth workbook / by Nancy Ashley. — 1st
Prentice Hall Press ed.
        p.   cm.
    ISBN 0-13-189382-3
    1. Dreams—Problems, exercises, etc.   2. Dreams—Miscellanea.
3. Seth—Views on dreams.   4. Spirit writings.   I. Title.
BF1091.A74   1990
154.6'3—dc20   89-48362
                                                                                CIP

Designed by Irving Perkins Associates

Manufactured in the United States of America

10   9   8   7   6   5   4   3   2   1

First Edition

For Clover

Contents

Introduction

Dreams: Why, What, and How

How real are dream events? What do dreams mean? How do they affect daily life? . . . Such issues . . . while obviously of concern, do not touch upon the greater events behind dream activity, or begin to touch upon the mysterious psychological actions that are behind the perception of any event . . . and the characteristics of energy, without which no action is possible.

The Nature of the Psyche, pp. 142–3.

The upsurge of interest in psychic phenomena over the past three decades reflects changing beliefs about the nature of reality. For five hundred years Western thinking was predominately materialistic: What you see and what you can measure is what you get—reality. Only recently, due paradoxically to the discoveries of physicists, the once heretical notion that material reality arises out of a nonmaterial source (perhaps even out of consciousness or mind) has gained ground. As the scientific community (by consensus, our experts on what to believe and what not to believe) comes out with such ideas, the public is not long in taking them up and trying them out.

Still, most scientists—perhaps feeling more heavily burdened than ever by their role as society's gurus and "lie detectors"—are reluctant to ascribe nonmaterial causes to phenomena like precognition or telekinesis. And while they may admit that not all cases of such can be explained away as coincidence, suggestion, or hallucination, they know that they themselves haven't experienced anything like their consciousness going into the future to preview events that haven't happened yet or their minds controlling matter at a distance. How could it be possible?

Yet, every night, that is what their consciousness does: It travels into the future, into the past, into other bodies, changes an object into a person, a person into an object, transports them instantly to a faraway place, and on and on. As does everyone else's consciousness. For that matter, it is not only at night this happens; it goes on all the time. The consciousness that we think of as us is such that it can focus in material reality, where it takes on identity as a three-dimensional being, while at the same time maintaining endless other identities and existences elsewhere, both "in" and "out" of matter. In our dreams we get in touch with this multidimensional aspect of ourselves.

Because of our still engrained materialistic beliefs, many of us have yet to be aware of so-called extrasensory phenomena while in full waking consciousness (though they happen all the time). Such occurrences as foretelling events or finding lost articles through "seeing" where they are make news precisely because they are unusual. People who report experiences of this kind to those of us who have not had them may be regarded as masterminds, kooks, or charlatans, depending on our bias. Whatever they are, they are not like most of us.

Yet even the most logical of empiricists, the type of people who have never once experienced a waking phenomenon for which they could not provide a rational explanation, will easily and openly admit that they dream. In most cases they don't remember their dreams, but they do remember that they dreamed, and that their consciousness acted in strange ways, in ways that could be described as, well, extrasensory. Yet they are not at all reluctant to admit this, knowing that everyone else shares that experience, knowing that when it comes to dreaming, we are all alike.

They can admit this because to them dreams are no more than pictures in the mind, akin to imaginings but more distorted—more like hallucinations. But while it is *not* all right to have hallucinations (if you're wide awake and seeing things that aren't there, something must be wrong with you), it *is* all right to have dreams. You're asleep, you're not participating in space-time, so you can let your mind conjure up images. Everyone does.

However, according to Seth, the world of dreams is just as real as the world of space and time. In fact, it is *more* real in that it contains more dimensions. In dreams we are more aware than when we are awake of the basic multidimensionality of consciousness, of our own multidimensionality as consciousnesses. Even so, because of our strong space-time orientation, when in the dream world we may tend to perceive that reality through a glass darkly, like a bemused and confused observer of a weird television show. Because we have decided that at most dreams present a distorted version of our own world in need of decoding, we fail to recognize the reflection of a basic reality out of which our own emerges. We fail to recognize that the events we encounter in dreams are half-materialized symbols of an underlying nonmaterial reality. We don't see that the events in dreams, far from being distorted versions of space-time occurrences, are instead events in the process of becoming materialized. Never does it occur to us that our reality is based on dream reality, not the other way around, that, rather than form dream events out of waking events, we form the events of our waking life through the mediation of our dreams.

Energy and Consciousness

On a "higher" level of materiality, where energy takes on visible form in space and time, the rules of science work perfectly. But not on the subatomic level.

Nuclear physicists have found that the tiny bits of energy within atoms called particles seem to have a "mind of their own," behaving in unpredictable ways that defy physical laws. They blink in and out of existence, create one another, communicate at a distance, go backward in time, seem to be in two places at once. The physicists have concluded that either human consciousness influences the behavior of the particles or that energy itself has a nonphysical property akin to consciousness.

According to Seth, energy is a nonphysical property that a latent consciousness developed in order to actualize itself. In space-time terms, there was a time when consciousness—All That Is—lay in abeyance, a vast glassy sea of psychological potential, but with no means to real-ize this: the original cosmic dilemma. The more All That Is dreamed of its potentialities, the more it *longed* to actualize them and so to express "out there" what was "in here." Strong desire grew into an unbelievably powerful agony, reaching an unbearable pitch and . . . consciousness exploded in a primordial Big Bang. In a process reflected in space-time by nuclear fission, an infinitude of "consciousness units" (mental entities out of which all physical matter is formed) split off from the original undivided whole, transforming consciousness into what it is today: both indivisible and separated, each tiniest bit of itself aware of its source but with its own unique perspective, propelled by the *energy of feeling* that gave it its birth as an individual into the constant action of being, out of a primal desire to know itself. Physical manifestation is but one of its infinite means.

As we've seen, like Seth, some physicists are saying that consciousness and energy are inextricably related: Science is approaching "mysticism" on that point. But scientists (most of them) still see energy and consciousness as a dichotomy: One is physical, the other, nonphysical. Though in one of science's explanations consciousness is viewed as a property of energy rather than a separate entity acting upon energy, still the assumption is that the one is physical, the other nonphysical. The scientists do not think in terms of nonphysical energy, much less in terms of physical consciousness.

But in Seth's view, energy/consciousness is like a vibratory spectrum, and physical form a range on that spectrum. Because energy is a property of consciousness, when energy breaks through into the material range, so too does consciousness. It isn't that consciousness exists as a nonphysical aspect of a physical structure but that consciousness (along with energy) is physicalized *as that structure*, as a form that consciousness takes in order to know itself. And it goes without saying that energy has its nonmaterial forms. Each thought, memory, and dream is imbued with energy, the nonphysical energy of *feeling*. If it were not for that feeling energy, consciousness would still be latent. In order to learn and create there must not only be something to be learned but the desire to do so. Everything began when an intense desire to know vaporized that glassy sea of undifferentiated meaning and set creativity in motion. Energy gave character to consciousness; it is through the energy inherent in meaning that we know it, that we know ourselves.

The Nature of the Psyche

Energy is consciousness in motion, impelled to form patterns so as to make itself "visible." Every unit of consciousness has its own particular viewpoint, giving it a sense of identity and significance, and at the same time it is energized to explore and expand its viewpoint through combination with other units of consciousness, forming gestalts. Gestalts form gestalts, and so on, not randomly, but through the attraction of like *significances*. Significance (or meaning or identity or psychological character) can be likened to an electromagnet, which draws to it particles with a positive charge and repels those with a negative charge. Like an electromagnet, consciousness units attract and repel one another through their similar or dissimilar significance, in this way exploring meaning.

The psyche, or whole self, is a conglomeration of energy gestalts with a portion of its energy focused in material reality. We perceive this portion as "us" (the ego) but it also includes reincarnational and probable selves (other egos). Reincarnational selves are versions of us in different time slots in the same universe; probable selves are versions of us in the same time slot in different universes—alternate space-times where alternate selves pursue roads not taken here. Together we form a gestalt of physically oriented energy, an ever-changing kaleidoscope of embodied consciousness: the total physical manifestation of the psyche at any one "time."

And of course the multidimensionality does not end there. Each "us," each ego, is in turn a composite of three forms of consciousness: that of the inner self, that of the ego, and that of the body. The term "inner self" applies to the portion of psychic consciousness participating in the ever-changing psychological reality from which space-time is created; the term "ego" applies to one of the myriad portions participating in the slow-moving play of materialized consciousness with its actors and scenery and props. Together they comprise what we think of as "our" consciousness in its different focuses and different roles.

The consciousness of the ego is physically oriented but entirely different from the physically oriented consciousness of the body. The ego experiences sight, sound, touch, taste, and smell. It responds to events emotionally according to its belief system and identifies itself as a body, but feels separate from its environment. The cells of the body, each of which is simultaneously conscious of itself as an entity and of its participation in an inseparable whole, don't experience emotions and sensations in the same way the ego does, but they have their own electromagnetic version. They respond literally to the ego's beliefs about the nature of reality and do what they can to create a physical version of those beliefs. Their role in dreaming is crucial, for it is on the cellular level of consciousness that psychological reality is converted into physical reality. It is because the cells dream along with "us" that we experience physical sensations when dreaming. In fact, in the dream state, the inner self, ego, and body consciousnesses to some extent merge, "recognizing" one another in a way that is rare when the ego is awake. They recognize they are all part of one another.

The brain enables us to operate in space-time by synchronizing physically oriented data for both the body and the ego. It blocks out much of the information coming from the inner self so the ego can maintain its narrow focus on physical reality, perceiving events one at a time with objects fixed in space like a series of snapshots. Relatively free of time and space constraints, body consciousness can handle much more information from the inner self. The ego tends to regard itself as the one possessing consciousness and the body as little more than a machine that needs its help in order to keep running. In fact, we have a lot to learn by tuning in to our body's natural knowing.

The kaleidoscope of physically oriented selves—reincarnational and probable versions of "us"—all share the consciousness of the inner self. This means of course that each of us is simultaneously the kaleidoscope and a part of the kaleidoscope itself. When immersed in space-time it's difficult to conceive of ourselves as part of a kaleidoscope of selves, much less to imagine ourselves as the kaleidoscope itself—as multidimensional beings existing simultaneously here and there and now and then, participating in countless physical realities (not even to mention here the nonphysical realities the psyche has a part in). But in our dreams, when freed of the usual space and time constraints, it seems natural that we simultaneously maintain our familiar identity as "us" and experience ourselves in different guises in different time periods. Awakening, we may forget that sense of familiarity and remember the dream as being about "someone else"—which, in space-time terms, is true. But whether we call them other entities, other selves, or other aspects of ourself, we meet them in dreams and cooperate in forming material reality.

The Nature of Dreams

In space-time terms, dreaming is what happens when consciousness "shifts gears," when the energy giving motion to consciousness changes focus. Energy gestalts group around significances, each creating a unique reality, each humming with its own particular intensity. The dream state, as a stage of transition between realities, is not a phenomenon limited to mankind (or earthkind). Every form of consciousness, physical and nonphysical, has states analogous to our sleep when perceptions shift and "reality" changes. In our case, dreams bridge material and nonmaterial reality, blending elements of both. If we view dreams from a waking perspective, they may seem distorted to us. In fact, they are a combination of realities, and through seeming distortions we glimpse the nature of other realities.

Dreams serve as intermediaries, making it possible for entities experiencing one reality to communicate with those experiencing another. While awake the entities participating within a chosen reality must (to varying extents) keep it in focus, but during sleep their attention can stray, and in fact needs to stray in order to glean the necessary information to keep the system in a state of constant creation. Some of that information comes from other entities within the same system, in our case not only from all other humans on earth but all other life forms. Other information comes from the "outside," from other realities, and provides the raw material (perceived as probable events) to use in reality creation.

In space-time, we all participate in the material reality of objects and actions, but have numerous languages to symbolize that reality. To someone who doesn't know Spanish, the word for "chair" is meaningless until translated, after which the Spanish reality becomes clear in the English reality. Similarly, all of "us"—the infinite manifestations of energized consciousness—have in common the nonmaterial reality of pure energy, but we have innumerable "languages" (realities, focuses on significance) that need to be translated in order for us to understand what this energy is like "there." Dreams do us that service, which is why Seth calls them "the language of the psyche." They translate one language of conscious energy into terms understandable in another.

Languages are known for their creativity. Even if we want to we cannot produce the same utterance twice. While the words may be the same, intonation, voice quality, timing, or some other aspect will differ, making each utterance a unique creation. When we translate a sentence from Spanish to English, we create a new reality, to some extent helping us to understand the reality of the Spanish but by no means re-creating it. Something is lost in translation, but gained—in the form of originality.

The same is true of our reality: Something is lost in the translation from another reality, but something of crucial importance is gained—a unique creation. From this perspective, dreams are not merely a means of translating the language of energy from one reality to another, but also the agency through which new realities are created.

How Events Are Formed

The psyche, as a conglomeration of energy gestalts having a particular psychological identity, continually attracts to it other similarly inclined energy in order to explore meaning and know itself. Physical manifestation is one means of exploration: What we see "out there" is at every point in time an updated version of the contents of the psyche in materialized form, its psychological characteristics clothed in chemicals.

It's as if part of us (the inner self) were on a continual journey into the psychological depths, sending back to another part of us (the ego) new ideas and mementos. Ranging far and deep into "the raw material of experience," we know the power and vitality of All That Is, the universe of meaning from which all "reality" is created, looking back and forward in time at our individual selves, at civilizations, involving ourselves in what other consciousnesses know and do, understanding all probabilities and their implications. At no "point" in this journey do we lose our sense of individuality, of our own "indestructible validity," but use it as "bait" to attract to us (and be attracted to) probable events (significances, raw experiences) appropriate to our identity.

Cellular consciousness takes a parallel journey, perceiving all probabilities in the nonphysical realm concerned with biochemical reactions and whatever is necessary for physical survival of the body under all possible circumstances (such as the effects of different beliefs). Seth calls these journeys we take the "predream" state.

Predream events are of course on an entirely different "wavelength" from space-time events. And so, as they "approach" space-time, they gradually shift wavelengths in the dream state, the data, from our perspective, becoming more specific than those on "higher" levels. During this process those many events that cannot be perceived on a lower level fall away.

At this point ego consciousness becomes involved. The inner self meets with the ego in the dream state, where portions of the consciousness of each overlap, enabling them to communicate more directly using elements of each consciousness. The probable events in the "mind" of the inner self are experienced in the "mind" of the ego. The events still have no physical shape—they are not "seen" or "heard."

The present desires, intentions, and beliefs of the ego are chemically coded within the body according to "significance." When in the dream state the ego and inner self focus on probable events that to some extent match these significances, chemical reactions are triggered in the dreaming body, which "runs through" these events so that, as they resonate within, the ego can get an idea of what it would be like to experience them in space-time. When we remember our dreams, it is these "distorted" events we remember. In most cases probable events get no further than this, as waking conflicts are worked out at this stage, leaving no need to actualize the events. We choose to actualize relatively few.

Certain events mesh totally with our expectations. We are highly attracted to their strong "felt significance." Our intense focus causes the events to resonate more strongly, triggering more reactions in the body's sensory apparatus, which processes the still largely psychological data into codes that will determine the nature of the events in space-time. (That is, a "probable event" might appear in space-time as a sound, an object, or a happening.) This is perhaps the most creative part of the process, with imagination playing a key role.

In several books, Seth mentions EE (electromagnetic energy) units, the "invisible breath of consciousness" that underlies matter. EE units give final shape to the events (now specifically coded within the body) so that they can break into space-time, where the ego will experience them with its senses as "out there" rather than "in here." For EE units to be activated requires yet more emotional intensity. It is the strong feeling energy of consciousness that gives birth to any reality (as it did in the Beginning). By emotional intensity, Seth does not mean vehement conscious desire or strong will and effort on the part of the ego, but rather an accumulation of significances, creating a powerfully resonating field of feeling, until . . . the Big Bang. Which of course is happening every microsecond of our existence as we continually "real-ize our dreams."

Expanding Waking Consciousness

According to Seth, our species is at the point in evolution now where we're ready to expand our waking consciousness, ready as a species to do what some individuals with ESP have shown us we can, ready to make more thorough use of our "psychic" abilities, to become more conscious creators of our reality. And a primary means of accomplishing this is through becoming thoroughly familiar with dream consciousness. As we've seen, dreams bridge material and nonmaterial reality, blending elements of both. In dreams we encounter events in the process of becoming materialized, getting a sense of the reality from which they emerge, getting a strong sense of connection to our source of creativity and power.

The more familiar we become with dream consciousness, both during and after dreams, the more we will come to see that the same consciousness that dreams also operates in space-time; it is the same consciousness, the same familiar "us," just operating according to the rules of a different reality. We will see that we are consciousness in whatever form it takes and that to a much greater extent than we do now, we can bring into our space-time experience a consciousness that is simultaneously aware of its three-dimensional role and of its power as a multidimensional being.

Thus, half of the exercises in this book are devoted to expanding the waking consciousness we know, stretching it out, and creating much less of a gap between waking and dreaming reality for us. What we do in dreams with our consciousness we can, to a much greater extent than is current, do in waking life.

1

Reasons for Resistance

. . . the conscious mind is able to handle much more dream recall than you allow.

The Nature of the Psyche, p. 193.

Dreams are essential to the maintenance of space-time, keeping the body and all other physical forms in place and operating, infusing the system with creativity, ensuring constant growth and change. Whether or not we remember our dreams, they do their work. So why try to remember them?

Seth suggests a number of reasons. Perhaps we have a physical difficulty. In our dreams we play out a number of scenarios, finding a good resolution of the difficulty, which is, however, dependent upon the waking self's cooperation. The next day we get an impulse to do something out of the ordinary, perhaps to eat a certain food, or to stay home from work and rest, or even to see a certain film that would give us new information and new beliefs to remedy the condition. These are probable events, waiting in the wings for materialization, needing the ego's conscious decision to actualize them. If we choose not to obey the impulse, the bodily condition may become more obvious, and more drastic solutions may be dreamed up until one way or another the challenge is met and the lesson learned.

If we are not used to tuning in to our inner self, either through dreams or through altering our usual waking consciousness in various ways, then we may not recognize its messages (such as impulses, hunches, and any out-of-the-ordinary conditions in the body). Thus we set up an unnecessary barrier between the inner and the outer, denying ourselves the natural wisdom of our greater self and making space-time a lot more difficult than it need be.

One reason to remember our dreams is so that we will become more aware and trusting of the messages coming through to us. In developing a sense of familiarity with the inner world and its different way of operating, and by becoming used to its lack of logic and juxtaposed images, we'll be more willing to entertain what may seem to be impossible or ridiculous notions. If we talk to others about their successes, we hear phrases like "I had this crazy idea" or "It seemed silly, but something told me to go for it" or "My head told me one thing, my guts another, and I decided to follow my guts." Inspiration always comes from within, and the more receptive to its strange-seeming messages we are, the more creative we'll be in our waking lives.

There are a number of other reasons for remembering our dreams. Since

1

dreams are where events are formed, remembering them keeps us in direct waking contact with that process. Since in dreams we know ourselves as multidimensional, richly creative beings, our memory of dreams gives us a conscious connection to those roots. Since within dreams we experience the unity of our being through a sensual and psychological melding, in our remembrance of dreams we can experience that meld. Remembering dreams helps us to understand daily life. Remembering dreams expands our waking consciousness. And finally, since dreams are downright fascinating, to remember them is to be fascinated anew.

If our dreams can do so much for us, why is it we "can't" remember them? Seth says it is more natural to remember them than not to. Why, then, do they evade us?

One reason could be the belief that the only true reality is the one that comes to us through our sensual experience, as epitomized by the expression "Seeing is believing." Then dream reality, bearing so little resemblance to waking reality, just seems too weird. We can't for one minute believe in the reality of our dream images because they don't mesh with the visual constraints of space-time. At worst, they are distorted versions of what we "know" to be the true reality; at best, metaphors. Because metaphors are not "concrete," whatever meaning they have is open to interpretation, and we prefer to stick with what we can know "for sure." Inner knowing and inner seeing—intuition—being suspect, we dismiss our dreams as weird and forget them.

With this attitude, of course, we can never hope to become more conscious within our dreams, since "conscious" to us means experiencing space-time through the senses, but the only way we can "come awake" within our dreams is to let go of our usual concept of space and time. Thus we're at an impasse, impeding our progress in understanding and working with dreams.

As children we may have been told not to daydream, clearly understanding the term to be derogatory, and "letting the mind wander" came to mean straying from true consciousness into an undesirable mental state. If we had "out of body" experiences, we may have come to worry that we couldn't find our way back. As adults we may now fear our dreams, fear losing "conscious control" within them and getting swept away into insanity, our consciousness annihilated. We do not seem to understand that quite the opposite is true: The more free and playful our awareness, the more our consciousness expands.

Another reason we may not remember our dreams could be that we have been instilled with the old Christian belief that man is inherently sinful and must be constantly on guard so as not to let that side take over and open a Pandora's box full of malevolence.

With such an attitude no wonder we fear what might be revealed through inner exploration. We may be most concerned with sexual imagery. Seth says sexuality is often the strongest area of energy people are connected with, and their self-image is dependent on their beliefs in this area. They may have encountered, or fear to encounter, dream images of masturbation, homosexual relations, or other sexual fantasies that their beliefs tell them are evil. Fearing to find out for sure that they are as depraved as they suspect, they "forget" their dreams. This may seem an overstatement; it *is* the last decade of the twentieth century, after all. But who of us has not once winced, inwardly or outwardly, over some thought we've had of ourselves, over something we've done that we don't like, that a "good" person wouldn't do? Our very perfectionism reflects the belief that we are imperfect and must work very hard to "improve."

Seth says the more directly we experience our inner self the less mysterious and frightening it is. Once we become familiar with its system of logic (and it *is* a logical system, associating data, not according to cause and effect or first and last, but via the emotional similarities called significances) we can then realize the so-called unconscious is not the chaotic repository of fearful imagery we've been led to believe but a highly organized, highly creative system sustaining and nourishing our space-time selves, we'll feel much more courageous and much more free to follow our impulses.

Another fear standing in the way of remembering dreams is that they might foretell a disaster that "comes true." The media abound with stories of people having dreamed about airplane crashes and other events before they happened. We tend to feel we'd rather not know about—and thus dread—a disaster when there's nothing we can do about it anyway. But any seemingly future event we dream about is a probability, not an actuality. It may never happen, especially if we are aware of the probability. In the next chapter we'll be looking at precognition and prediction in detail.

A final reason we may not remember our dreams could be that we're afraid if we *do* remember them and don't write them down, or write them down but don't do any further thinking about them, we'll feel guilty because we're "supposed to" get something out of them. Seth once told Rob (Jane Roberts's husband) that he hadn't been remembering his dreams lately because he didn't want to take the time to write them down and analyze them. I've experienced the same resistance. This comes from being too conscientious and serious.

Seth has much to say about the creative, playful quality of dreams. As long as we explore them with deadly seriousness they'll tend to escape us, either because we force them into space-time terms or because we "forget" them. If, rather than trying to bring dream interpretation down to our level, we imaginatively enter the more free-ranging dream reality, we'll have better results and it won't seem like an arduous chore we feel resistant to.

Exercise #1

Become a record keeper. In one notebook write down your dreams. Even if all you remember are fragments, write them down and date them. In another notebook or on small notepads all over the house, in the car, at the workplace, write down your random thoughts and daydreams, your hunches and impulses. Take note of body symptoms—an ache, a rash, tiredness under certain circumstances. Simply by deciding to do this you will begin to notice stray thoughts off to the side of official reality, subtle signals from the body. When watching TV or reading, listening to others talk or looking at a view, notice what stands out for you and how your body feels. As soon as possible make a record of it.

You really cannot do too much record keeping. Your notes continue to be of value years after they are made, because each time you read them, you approach them as a new you and get new insights and inspiration from them. By reviewing them periodically you'll come to see how much your life is guided by these messages from your inner being.

I recently reread a dream I had in July of 1988. One minor character I didn't pay much attention to at the time I had the dream was a screenplay writer who didn't then want to show his scripts to anyone. I identified with the character as a fellow writer, but the kind of writing he was doing didn't strike me then. But when I read through the dream just over a year later, I realized the dream was precognitive. The character was myself, a screenplay-writer-to-be, who, a few months after having the dream, "just happened" to take a screenwriting class, discovered I was a natural at that kind of writing, and found a way to branch out just as I'd hoped. I would not have remembered this dream had I not recorded it, and thus would have missed the thrill of affirmation when rereading it later.

It is important to be playful in your record keeping, approaching it with curiosity rather than something to prove. You might want to cut out colorful pictures from magazines and make collages as you go along. You might want to use a different color of pen for each book or each mood. You might try writing backhand in one place and with a forward slant somewhere else. You might write in verse, or make a poster of what you write. The idea is to make record keeping fun. You'll find it valuable in doing many of these exercises, and you should continue your notebook after completing this workbook.

Exercise #2

The beliefs listed below may create resistance to dream recall. Check those you agree with in any way. Then examine your emotional reaction to each belief. Allow the emotion to generate other beliefs you associate with it. In your imagination exaggerate the beliefs and intensify the emotions to the point where they become ridiculously melodramatic, to the point where they no longer seem real.

1. Dreams are not real.
2. Dreams are a distortion of normal waking life.
3. I distrust anything that is not concrete.
4. Dreams are too weird for me to understand.
5. When we are dreaming we are not conscious.
6. It is impossible to be conscious while dreaming.
7. Altered states of consciousness are scary.
8. Any state of consciousness other than that of normal waking reality is undesirable.
9. Daydreaming is a big waste of time.
10. We shouldn't let our minds wander.
11. To the extent that we let our minds wander we are less capable and efficient than we should be.
12. While dreaming we are out of conscious control.
13. If I get into my dream too much, I might go insane.
14. Consciousness can be annihilated if we're not careful.
15. I'm not so sure I want to know myself better.
16. We are all sinners.
17. We must discipline ourselves to keep from falling into evil ways.
18. I don't really think I'm a very good lover and I don't want to find out why.
19. I may not be as well adjusted as I think I am.
20. If I have a dream that I'm a homosexual, that means I am one.
21. I am a homosexual and I'm afraid my dreams will tell me that's bad.
22. I had a dream I was masturbating; there must be something wrong with me.
23. I dreamed I made it with an animal. Isn't that awful?
24. It's a continual battle to be a good person.
25. Dreams aren't logical and organized enough to help me improve myself.

26. Everyone knows the unconscious is filled with darkness and terror.
27. I don't want to remember a nightmare.
28. There's no way to make sense of dreams since there's no logic to them.
29. What if I dream about a disaster and then it happens?
30. I once dreamed about a disaster and it happened. I dread having that experience again.
31. Dreams about the future always happen.
32. I'd rather not know the future since I can't do anything about it anyway.
33. Dream study must be taken very seriously indeed.
34. I just don't have the time to write down and work with my dreams.
35. It's important to fully understand our dreams and how they relate to our daily reality.
36. Other people's dreams are so much more interesting than mine.
37. Other people seem to be a lot better at interpreting their dreams than I am.
38. I've somehow got to set aside a large block of time and use it exclusively for working with dreams, even if it means giving up fun things to do.
39. My dreams are never very interesting anyway.
40. I'm just not good at working with dreams.
41. I'm not a very intuitive person.
42. How can you be sure your intuitions are correct?
43. People would think I was crazy if I told them I decided to do something because of a dream.
44. I'm afraid if I follow my impulses I'll get into trouble.
45. I've asked for guidance from my dreams and nothing happened.

Exercise #3

Whether or not we remember our dreams, they do their work. Often, we're none the wiser, taking very much for granted their role in our lives, never wondering where new ideas come from, or solutions to problems, or for that matter, ordinary events. It never occurs to us that our beliefs have changed over the years, usually without our noticing it, because of new information from the dream state. Simply bringing to conscious awareness the many services dreams provide will lessen our resistance to remembering them.

1. Recall some important decisions you've made lately. How did you decide? Think especially of occasions when you couldn't make up your mind for a while and then all of a sudden could. What happened?
2. What are some beliefs you used to have that you don't have now? How did you change your mind? Where did the information come from?
3. Can you remember having a bothersome bodily condition that spontaneously disappeared? Did you consciously cure yourself, or was the cure an "unconscious" process?
4. Think of some impulses you've recognized and followed through on. How did you get them?
5. If you have found "explanations" other than dreams for a lot of the above, then you are most likely to some extent dream resistant. Decide to suspend your doubts and affirm your dreams. Tell yourself from now on you will recognize the work that they do, and appreciate them for it.

Exercise #4

If you still find that your dreams totally elude you, write your own waking dream. Simply tell yourself you are going to write down a dream, let your imagination take over, and begin writing. Don't try to plan or organize what you're going to say, just let it flow. Do this regularly. You'll be surprised at how easy it is to slip into a state of altered consciousness akin to dreaming, and at how familiar this state really is. If anything can break down resistance to remembering your dreams, this exercise will. And it's fun.

The first time I did this exercise, this is what I wrote:

> I am talking to some people. We are in a room. I look out the window, and as I do so, I rise and fly out to what I see. Wherever I look I somehow "travel" there, *am* there. A tree in the distance is suddenly before me, I am in it and part of it. I look up at the clouds—I AM the clouds—as if the act of sensing something creates that thing and ME.
>
> From the clouds I look down on the sea, and I AM the sea. I lap up on the beach and become the sand. It tickles, those little crabs burrowing in me! I am a crab. I scuttle across the bumpy sand at lightning speed, knowing where my hole is, knowing where every single other crab is, seeing those crabs, and I am crabkind, all of the crabs together, the network of crabs. And we perceive an enormous entity approaching our network and we are that entity—a human being, an enormous giant who sees the sand grains not as bumps but as fine soft powder, and I am the sand once again, and I am cool underneath and warm on the surface, and the sea washes over me and I am that washing and that lap sound and now I am the sound, the collective sound of all the waves on the reef, and I'm the reef, teeming with life, and all those lives are a network, a community. I am that community. (And I awaken to desk, yellow lamplight, and cats sprawled around.)

Exercise #5

Most of us, at least occasionally, remember a dream, but those who regularly remember them are in the *habit* of doing so. They are in the habit of thinking positively about dreams, of looking to them for guidance, of trusting in their wisdom—and of remembering and writing them down to begin with. Below are some actions you can take that will develop into habits if repeated consistently. It usually takes about three weeks to form a habit, before which you may be tempted to skip the activity every now and again, but after which you will feel a bit uncomfortable if you do.

1. Make a tape to play every night, suggesting you will remember your dreams, repeating one to five positive beliefs about dreaming.
2. Suggest to yourself at bedtime that you are going to remember your dreams. Keep repeating the suggestion until you fall asleep.
3. Keep a notepad and pen by your bed. Upon awakening immediately write something down, whatever comes to mind, even if it does not seem to you to be a dream, even if it seems nonsensical, vague, or banal. Form the habit of writing something every morning.
4. Arrange with a friend or family member to share dreams on a regular basis—no less than once a week. Knowing that person is expecting you to have a dream to tell will motivate you to remember.
5. Join a dream group, or form your own.
6. Change your wake/sleep patterns. Sleep for a while in the late afternoon and a shorter period at night. This brings the waking and sleeping states closer together and enhances recall.

Exercise #6

Space-time was created and continues to be created out of the strong feelings of meaningfulness that Seth calls significance, the center of an intense focus. Each of us participating in space-time is at once a part of the ever-changing significance of space-time and a uniquely significant focus of our own.

"Feeling tones" is the term Seth uses to describe the resonance of meaning within us, the sound of our significance, the chords of our identity, the surge of consciousness flowing into physical experience as it seeks to real-ize meaning. They are our signature as a feeling, living being. These tones determine the overall emotional quality of our life, our attitude toward ourselves and life in general. And, emanating from the deepest part of our being, these tones lie beneath the transitory emotions of day-to-day life. They are our creative core, the essence from which our body is formed.

Once we become aware of the power, strength, and durability of our own "inner voice," we can go courageously into the deeper realities of our being feeling safe and protected; we can explore our dreams joyously and playfully while we are grounded in our being.

Spend a few minutes every day getting in touch with this inner voice, with this deep chord of yourself; feel the significance that is you, your identity. Sit quietly with your eyes closed and feel deep inside to the core of your being. Ask your dreams, too, to attune you with the deep vibrations of your person-hood.

2

Precognition and Significance, Prediction and Imagination

. . . you are aware of some future events before they happen . . . whether or not you succeed in conscious prediction.

The Nature of the Psyche, p. 53.

Sue Watkins's latest book, *Dreaming Myself, Dreaming a Town* is (among other things) a study of precognition, which Sue views as a natural biological function we can become more aware of through practice. Our initial awareness of the ubiquity of precognition may come from a source like *Ripley's Believe It or Not,* such as Sue found in a 1982 newspaper:

THERE WERE FOREWARNINGS
AT THREE MILE ISLAND!
A dozen residents in the area of the March 1979
nuclear reactor accident in Pennsylvania,
according to Larry E. Arnold, director of the
Harrisburg, Pa., ParaScience International,
independently "EXPERIENCED THE SAME
PROPHETIC NIGHTMARE IN WHICH THEY
SAW THE COOLING TOWERS OF THREE
MILE ISLAND GLOWING DEEP RED, WITH
LIGHTNING CRACKLING ALL AROUND."*

Such accounts have no credence in scientific circles because they come after the fact and could be a result of suggestion, among other possibilities. Even cases of dreams reported *before* the event are usually written off as "coincidence," since the only other alternative is to admit the possibility of precognition, when "everyone knows" we cannot see something that hasn't yet happened.

Still, following every public event comes a smattering of reports like the one above. Since people don't want to risk being labeled crackpots, many such dreams doubtless go unreported, though Sue had no trouble getting people in her small village of Dundee, New York, to share dreams with her. Many

---

* Sue Watkins, *Dreaming Myself, Dreaming a Town* (New York: Kendall Enterprises, 1989), p. 106.

reported dreaming about the death of a villager before it happened, as well as dreams they had about their own lives that later "came true." This was no surprise to Sue, who for years has been keeping careful records of her own dreams, and who wrote about precognitive dreams, both public and private, in *Conversations with Seth*. Jane Roberts, too, in *The Coming of Seth* and elsewhere, has told of precognitive dreams.

According to Seth, such dreams are not simply common, they're universal. We have them, but may not be aware of them, either because we don't remember them or because we don't realize that the material, under its "disguise," is precognitive, not seeing the connection between the dream event and a later event in space-time. It may be that the waking event occurs months or years later when the not especially memorable dream is forgotten, or, more likely, that dream reality is so different from space-time it can rarely if ever be taken "literally." And, in the case of public events, each dreamer may supply just a piece of the puzzle, which only when compared with a number of other dreams about the same event will hint at the full picture.

Take, for example, the dreams about the death of the villager in Sue's book. Donald, the person who died, fell off a sailboat into a lake on a dark, foggy night, never to be seen again. On hearing of the accident the next day, Sue thought of her gloomy dream of the previous night about a diving bell descending into almost bottomless depths, among undersea canyons and caves. (The lake where Donald was lost is very deep and, because of its jagged canyons and caves, considered dangerous for divers and swimmers.) Later that day a man told Sue his dream about a big dark rowboat soundlessly tipping and breaking someone's arm; another person about sinking fully dressed into a swimming pool while looking up at the disappearing sunlight and feeling sad; another about standing in the fog at the lake waiting for friends to return from a boat ride; and another about simply a feeling of doom and disaster. As the days passed, more dreams came in, each in some way contributing to an overall picture, leading Sue to speculate whether, if she had the dreams of all 1,632 residents of Dundee, she'd have the complete account of the occurrence.

Whether mass event or private, the viewpoint of each person involved will of course be different. While it may appear that everyone experiences a given event in more or less the same fashion, our inner experiencing of it is as unique as our individuality, and our dreams faithfully reflect that inner experience. In this sense (as well as in others) dreams are closer to the reality of the event than the space-time version; in this sense they are more "literal." Let's look at an entry from my dream journal, dated August 15, 1988.

> Suddenly we are going to have a party and I buy food for it. R, who is in on the party and splitting the costs with me, buys a whole slew of stuff, much more than is needed, including some salami and a couple of big wooden

boxes of cheese. I take one of the boxes and squeeze it and the cheese way down into a small shape so it doesn't take up much space, so it isn't inflated, "letting the air out of it." It isn't as grandiose and showy as before. Then I think, *I don't want to reimburse R since she owes me money anyway.*

Here is what happened a day later: Some friends dropped over and we decided to have a barbecue at my house the following night for a mutual friend who was visiting briefly. We decided to have hamburgers, and they said they would pick up the meat and buns. "Just in case," I bought enough hamburger and buns to feed everyone, figuring it was better to have too much than not enough. When they arrived, they had not picked up any supplies and seemed not to remember the plan. One of them, disappointed that it was to be hamburgers when I am known for my good cooking, looked in the refrigerator and said, "Can we have cheeseburgers, at least? There's plenty of cheese," whereupon another one, saying he was ravenous, asked if he could have some of the cheese right away, as well as some salami he saw in there. Wanting them to contribute something, I sent them to the store for lettuce, ketchup, and wine.

Obviously, the dream is not a literal account of what happened later, but the two versions resemble one another in certain concrete ways—party, friends, splitting expenses, cheese, salami. However, the dream goes deeper, making "visible" (in the cheesebox-squeezing incident, for instance) my *feelings* about the event—its *significance* to me. Anyone reading the dream can see it is not really about a party so much as it is about my feeling of ambivalence toward generosity and sharing. On the other hand, those at the space-time event probably had no conscious awareness what the purpose, theme, and significance of the party were for me—why I was attracted to and created the situation. However, if they themselves had dreamed of the incident, they would undoubtedly have reached the heart of the matter, each in his or her own way. This was clear with the dreams on drowning mentioned earlier. Sue commented especially on how the feelings harmonized, despite the individuality of the dreams. Those who in some way participated in the drowning episode were attracted to the event through a shared area of significance. And I am sure that those who participated in the party were attracted to an underlying significance they wanted to explore in space-time from their own perspective.

It is significance, so obvious to us in dreams, that clues us in on future events in space-time. As Seth says, "Predictability is simply another word for significance." To the extent that we are aware in waking life of what is significant to us (what we are drawn to, what we have strong feelings about) we can predict the nature of the events we will draw to us.

Consciousness in its "pure" form is unpredictable, having no restrictions, no rules—total freedom of choice. And it is precisely this freedom of choice that leads to predictability. In its desire to know and express itself, and in its freedom to do so, consciousness looks about and finds a portion of itself significant. It then chooses to focus in on this significance, thus creating a system of "reality." In this sense each of us (the "ego-us" in space-time) is both a focus of consciousness (a significance) and a system of reality (an ever-changing and unique interpretation of that significance).

This of course is also true of a cell, the earth, our psyche, and so on. Meaning exploring meaning in every possible way. Seth says that as we "mature" we form a larger framework of identity, just as the consciousness of a given cell eventually evolves into the consciousness of an organ, experiencing its reality (and significance) from that "larger" viewpoint and leaving behind the cell's significance pattern for other consciousnesses to explore and expand upon in an entirely different way. Since every cell in the body emerges from the single cell created by sperm and egg, every cell contains within it the knowledge of how to create an entire body. Analogously, each of us, a seed of consciousness continually choosing its focus, contains the knowledge of our source. Perhaps every consciousness unit eventually ends up creating its own version of All That Is!

To some extent, then, we can forecast events for ourselves and the world through listening to the voice of significance within (especially dreams), through sensing what we feel attracted to (whether or not we like it), and what we expect out there in the world. Each sensed significance, each attraction, each expectation is a "realized" event to the psyche (whose consciousness, of which we are a part, has a larger focus, like an organ as compared to a cell). But to us in space-time the events are probable, and therein lies the rub.

Predictions about anything are based upon the strongest probabilities at any point in time, and event forming is no exception. Even with perfect knowledge and understanding of our beliefs, desires, and intentions we could not at any point in time make predictions about the future with anything approaching 100 percent accuracy, simply because our beliefs, desires, and intentions—our sense of what is significant—constantly change with new experience. The very act of observing something changes both object and observer, as scientists have shown. While we may be predictable (which gives us character), we are not predestined (which would make us automatons). No matter how dire a situation we're in, we always have a choice. Seth talks about people who in the midst of a serious illness suddenly take on a belief in good health (the result of an insightful dream and/or conscious focus on the desired belief), whereupon their body quickly returns to normal as new messages are passed on to the cells in keeping with this new picture, as new memories replace old ones, creating a new past in harmony with the changed present, as a new future, reflecting the changes, substitutes for the previous one.

With each new event in our lives, with each new present we create, we also create a new past and a new future. Since events are nothing more or less than conscious energy, each with its own identifiable significance, and since conscious energy, in toto, is All That Is, it then follows that this conscious energy exists now. It is not waiting in the wings to be created in some probable future nor is it standing on the sidelines, a used-up past. Past events are simply significances we have already focused on in this lifetime. They continue to have a life of their own, enriched and expanded through their interaction with us as we are with them. Future events are those we have yet to focus on but with which we are continually interacting, encountering one another in hopes, fantasies, and dreams. (As well as in worries, doubts, and desires for revenge.)

Which brings up the role of imagination in creating our reality. Seth says imagination is the form of waking consciousness closest to dream consciousness. By paying more conscious attention to what we imagine we can learn a lot about our beliefs and expectations, since we use the imagination as a waking playground for future scenarios. And in the creative play of our imagination is a reflection of dream reality, where, freed of space and time constraints, images flow directly out of our focus upon significance.

In a sense, the imagination is an extension of the dream state, allowing us, awake, to view the often "impossible" events of dreams, motivating us consciously to be creative, temporarily to let go of a belief in the impossibility of the image and see what we can do with it. A lot of inventions have come into the system via that route. But imagined events (whether the event is running the four-minute mile, once considered impossible, or the creation of a space-ship exceeding the speed of light, still considered so) are different from dream images in that they are more fleshed out so as to fit within the parameters of space-time. In other words, whatever we can imagine to be the case *can* be the case; our imagination is the repository of all space-time possibilities. But generally during any historical period we will all work with a given set of possibilities and look upon others as impossible—"only a dream." These possibilities have to wait their time—or perhaps already had their time. Seth says at one time gods fighting in the sky was a reality for us. People weren't considered insane if they experienced a space-time reality in which such things happened. It may be that fairies and leprechauns at one time were real too. Today we do not believe such "superstitious nonsense," though we enjoy reading imaginative novels or seeing television shows about situations we agree are outside the realm of possibility—just as earlier people agreed that such imagined phenomena as television or automobiles were not possible.

We find it difficult to conceive of the idea that what we "know" to be real is but our creation, once a figment of the imagination, a dream. Evolution was an imaginative construct until we decided to real-ize it. Before evolution became an almost universal belief, people experienced reality in a different fashion. It wasn't that they were ignorant of the way the world "really" worked;

it simply didn't work that way. However, once we came to view the universe as evolutionary, it cooperated, behaving the way we expected it to, offering up "proof" of our belief.

Humans have developed the faculty of imagination way beyond that of other earth creatures. It is our specialty, this faculty to envision and bring into space-time what other beings in their innocent acceptance of nature never once turn their minds to. Yet, as with dreams, we still fail to understand the connection between imagination and reality-creation, still fail to give it credit. Most of the time we are not even aware imagination is operating, and so we don't see that it follows along with our most entrenched beliefs, continually conjuring up new situations whereby to show them off. If we believe we are not safe, our imagination will faithfully run through the present possibilities around that belief, keeping us focused on it, assuring the continued appearance of unsafeness in our reality. Why not instead consciously enlist the imagination as a means of trying out new, positive ideas, actively visualizing situations that fit them, and thus set up new beliefs and expectations? Since the imagination is so closely allied with the dream state, where our reality is created, why not make use of this tool in waking life, becoming more conscious reality creators?

Exercise #7

Try your hand at prediction. Simply sit down with a notebook, write "Predictions for the Next Twenty-four Hours" (or "the Next Week"), and the date. Then write a "1" and see what happens. Write down whatever comes to mind in a word, phrase, or sentence. Then go to "2" and "3" and on until nothing more comes. Don't try to "make sense" of what you write and don't judge it; don't embellish it or change it. Be playful and curious, and don't worry whether you will "succeed."

The next day or the next week, check your predictions out one by one, asking yourself whether anything showed up in your reality in keeping with the prediction. Also check your dream notebook and your other notebooks of random daytime thoughts to see if there is a match—to see if you unknowingly "predicted" the event elsewhere. You will probably find the predictions that did "come true" were no big deal, just ordinary events in your life, fitting so snugly into your daily reality that you might not have given them a thought except for this exercise.

Jane Roberts in *How to Develop Your ESP Power* talks about her own results in writing down predictions:

> *Prediction for November 19*—a switch of days.—On this same day I received first a letter and then a phone call from my in-laws, who twice switched the date for a previously made engagement.
> *Prediction for November 20*—unexpected invitation.—On this date a friend dropped in to invite us to dinner. We had not seen her in months. Just before she knocked at the door I was strongly thinking about her.
> *Prediction for December 17*—woman in polka-dot dress; a study in reactions. —On this date a couple we know visited us unexpectedly. The woman wore a polka-dot dress. As we sat chatting, our attention was caught by the bizarre behavior of a child in the street . . ."*

And so on. She describes many more incidents that related to her earlier predictions and that in some cases she dreamed about as well. She also described an out of the ordinary event involving the accident of an elderly tenant in her apartment building that both she and her husband, Rob, had foreseen.

If you do this exercise over a period of time, you may see a pattern in which certain types of incidents are easier for you to predict than others, indicating perhaps that you are more consciously aware of your "sensed significance" in these areas than in others, or perhaps that your feelings (and thus beliefs) are more fixed in these areas, creating stronger probabilities, higher predictability.

* Jane Roberts, *How to Develop Your ESP Power* (New York: Fell Publishers, 1982), pps. 151–2.

Exercise #8

What is referred to in space-time as a cause-effect relationship Seth calls a "heavy-handed significance." In other words, two events occur together, one after the other, because we *strongly expect* them to—the felt significance of the first event is "completed" by the occurrence of the second event. It is around events of this kind, then, that we can make the most accurate predictions and at the same time discover some ingrained beliefs we have about the nature of our reality. Answer the following questions with what first comes to mind, not trying to be reasonable or "correct." In most cases you will initially come up with feelings. These will then lead you to your expectations/beliefs about reality in each situation, and then to some "most likely" predictions. Do this playfully and exaggerate all you want.

1. What if I got really angry at X?
2. What if I can't do the job?
3. What if I disagree?
4. What if I don't achieve as much as X does?
5. What if the job I do is not good enough?
6. What if they don't get punished for their wrongdoing?
7. What if *I* don't?
8. What if they don't realize they're wrong?
9. What if *I* don't?
10. What if everything is going wrong for me?
11. What if everything is going right?
12. What if I don't get what I want?
13. What if I do?
14. What if X keeps causing me trouble?
15. What if they won't do what I say?
16. What if I don't do what I'm supposed to do?
17. What if there could be danger involved?
18. What if I'm not worried about it?
19. What if life isn't easy?
20. What if I'm supposed to do a boring task?
21. What if I let others take care of me?
22. What if others expect me to take care of them?
23. What if I had a rotten childhood?
24. What if I've never had a lasting sexual relationship?
25. What if I leave this relationship?
26. What if I'm alone?

27. What if I meet someone else?
28. What if we can't get along?
29. What if he/she does not change?
30. What if they won't listen to me?
31. What if I can't come up with a solution right away?
32. What if there's no solution?
33. What if I just give up?
34. What if it's risky to change?
35. What if it's easier not to do anything?
36. What if I take the wrong action?

If you don't like some of the expectations you came up with, realize you can change them by vividly imagining different outcomes. Dramatize these, feel them, take them into your dreams, and real-ize them!

Exercise #9

Some years ago everyone believed it was impossible to run a mile in under four minutes. Then along came Roger Bannister who did it. Today athletes regularly break that once legendary barrier.

As with any other dreamed-of or imagined desires, the "barrier" was a belief and that's all. We *can* have what we desire, but only if we believe we can.

1. Make a list of your "impossible" desires, and after each one give the reasons you can't have it. Be playful and exaggerate as much as you can. In some cases you may find that you don't really desire whatever it is, or that having it means giving up something you now treasure. Others you may still desire and still be sure there is no way you can have them. Choose the "easiest" one and every day for three weeks imagine yourself having it. Suspend for that time your belief in impossibility and let yourself have what you want, feel yourself enjoying it—really get into it. Every night ask for a dream in which you are real-izing that desire. At the end of three weeks check out your reality for progress. Notice little things. If your desire is for someone to love, then the presence of just one new friend in your life is evidence that you're approaching the mark. More than likely, as you imagined your situation you found your desire slowly changing its form to more closely harmonize with your underlying feelings. It may be that what you really wanted was not a thing, not an achievement, but simply a feeling, and that through your imaginings you have learned how to feel that way and have let go of believing that feeling needs to come in a certain form.

2. What do you desire for the world to make it a better, happier place for everyone? What belief barriers stand in the way? How many of these beliefs do you personally have? Use your dreams and imagination to change them one by one.

Exercise #10

Make a list of "facts" about yourself: sex, age, race, parents, physical condition, marital status, whether you have children, how much education, the job you do, where you live, friends, activities, political stance.

Each one of these "facts" represents a strong focus of great significance to us, and as such an area around which we have relatively fixed beliefs. "As a female I should do this and not do that" or "Being a diabetic, I have certain limitations" or "I'm too old to do that." Think of some beliefs about yourself in these areas.

We tend to get bogged down in the various roles we play so well, forgetting we created them in the first place. A good way to remind ourselves of this is to imagine being the opposite, taking on an entirely different role. Not only does this remind us that we are much more than the role we play, but that we can expand our present role to include abilities we may have ruled out for ourselves through our stereotyped beliefs. We'll also discover beliefs we have about how our opposite should be.

Choose an area of your life with which you feel dissatisfied. Imagine yourself as the opposite and playfully act out your expectations of someone in that role. Summon up the feelings of that person, letting them flow through your body. Become that person and his or her beliefs. Hold that focus for a while and then gradually shift it back to yourself, gradually bring back the familiar feeling of yourself.

Seth says an imaginative experiment like this (as with dreams) will actually bring about neurological changes in your body, creating an expanded blueprint of yourself that includes the feelings and abilities you experienced in your imagination, and you can summon these to you anytime simply by recalling how they felt. The more you do so the more integrated and developed they will become.

Exercise #11

The difference between daydreams and waking dreams (of the sort you will be doing in this workbook) is that daydreams are passive and waking dreams are active. We're barely conscious of daydreams though they happen all the time. It's as if part of our mind, not needed fully in space-time, takes a vacation and goes off imagining. We don't fully participate in them as we do in waking dreams, when the imagination is active.

Jung came to the conclusion that active imagination was the most powerful tool for self-discovery, even more powerful than dreams. Active imagination is indeed a powerful tool, but since it is an extension of dream consciousness, it cannot be considered more powerful than something it is a part of. We need to stop thinking in terms of "conscious" and "unconscious," thus setting up a barrier that does not exist. Dreaming is simply a form that consciousness takes, and even within dreams consciousness has different forms, or stages, as it shifts "down" from nonmaterial awareness to material—as does waking consciousness, depending on its focus. We use our minds differently when surfing twenty-foot waves than we do when waiting in line at the bank. The form of waking consciousness closest to that of dream consciousness is imagination—active imagination with the mind and the body both involved. Seth has said that exercising our imagination in this way will enhance our dreams, and they will in turn enhance our imagination. The false distinction we have set up between waking and sleeping consciousness will break down as we recognize that the waking self and the sleeping self are the same self, the same consciousness in different modes.

Write a waking dream. This time try your hand at a precognitive one. Imagine yourself *dreaming about* yourself tomorrow as you go through your usual routine. Then just let the images flow. Don't censor it and don't try too hard. Be playful. When finished, put it aside without reading it. Wait until tomorrow's over before you do.

3

Association, Symbols, and the Emotions: Significance Revisited

When you understand how your own associations work, then you will be in a much better position to interpret your own dreams . . .

The Nature of the Psyche, p. 48.

As waking beings we live in two realities at once—the material reality of space-time, experienced through our senses, and the nonmaterial reality of the mind, experienced through our thoughts and emotions. Whatever we taste, touch, hear, see, or smell we simultaneously think and have feelings about. Some sensual experiences, such as those involved in competitive sports, so absorb us we can have little awareness of our thoughts and emotions at the time. Others, such as those involved in routine repetitive chores, absorb us very little. Still, we hardly notice as our mind wanders all over time and space while we stand at the sink doing dishes. In general we notice our sensual reality much more than we do our accompanying psychological reality, and when we do become aware of our thoughts and feelings, we see them as extraneous to or resulting from space-time experience.

This attitude—that material reality is primary and psychological reality, secondary—is very much ingrained, even I suspect in many of us who have intellectually accepted the idea that we create our physical reality through our thoughts, beliefs, and expectations. We are so very caught up in this 3-D technicolor living breathing creation of ours, we forget we are its creators, like a playwright so into his characters he's unconscious of simultaneously writing the play.

Because of this orientation, we see reality as organized in a particular way. Get up, brush teeth, make coffee, get dressed, get in car, go to work—the events following one another in time, the objects staying put in space. This is our official reality, what we focus our awareness on. At the same time our senses are recording all this, our minds are organizing the "same" experience in an entirely different way, associating the perceived objects and events, not in terms of when or where they are occurring, but in terms of their *felt meaning*, fitting them into a pattern of *significance*.

Thus, an object experienced in space-time—a fragrant pink rose, say—

will be experienced psychologically as tenderness (or sadness, or longing, or whatever) and associated with all other symbols (events, objects, whatever) that in our own very personal "filing system" signify that quality. The sensual event of the rose is then at the same time a psychological event of deep significance, adding to an area of meaning within our psyche. Through the space-time event, the psyche as a whole knows itself better, which changes it. If we encounter the same rose a few minutes later, its meaning will be felt again in a slightly different way, and add to our inner knowing once again. Or, its meaning could be felt in an entirely different way the second time (say, because of a feared spider crawling across it) and could be associated with another, entirely different area of significance (disillusionment, perhaps) and "filed" there so as to increase our inner understanding of *that*. And from then on, perhaps, the felt meaning of any rose will be disillusionment. Our sensually oriented selves, having forgotten the spider incident, may wonder why roses all of a sudden don't have the appeal they once did.

Though we could not operate in space-time if we were consciously aware of all the mental associations we make, still, we could be more aware than we are. We're in the habit of noticing our temporal and spatial perceptions and not of noticing what they symbolize to us, or what their significance is. As we look at a rose we see its shape and color, notice its position on the plant, are aware of the plant being in a next door garden and that the time of day is morning. But we may not notice that our mind is associating thus: "I love my Rose Milk hand lotion, and I had a pink dress when I was eight, and Grandma's mashed potatoes were something special, and yesterday's clouds and that poem I read and Northern California, wine, the Beatles, skyscrapers, the sea crashing in, tissue paper, Christmas 1972, smiles, and it all fits together somehow!" We may be aware of liking the rose but we're not aware of why, of how it fits into a pattern of significance. We'd find it laughable if someone said roses and mashed potatoes had anything in common even if we were aware of liking potatoes too. We're not used to associating things that way.

Seth calls this felt sense of meaning direct knowing, and we've all experienced it consciously from time to time. It may be a gentle joy at the way everything suddenly seems to fall into place, or a jolt when our reasons for acting a certain way become clear. Artists may experience it as inspiration, others as the voice of God. Depending on our beliefs, we may feel happy about it or we may feel afraid, but we'll know that we know, at least for the moment. And in that moment of "altered" consciousness we are aware of ourselves as much more than the waking selves of normal space-time experience, aware of ourselves as having deep psychic roots, which sustain and nourish us.

We can train ourselves to become more aware of our psychological reality without neglecting our sensual experience. It is not a matter of one mode or the other but rather of enriching our sensual experience through our conscious awareness of what it means, how it resonates within as it is happening without. Not only would such an expanded awareness enhance our experience of waking reality, but also we would better understand our dreams. Like waking consciousness, dream consciousness is a combination of sensual and psychological experience. But since in dreams there's no necessity to manipulate within space-time, the psychological component takes precedence, with events and objects organized according to significance. That is why dreams seem disjointed to us, with objects suddenly disappearing or changing form, and past, present, and future all mixed in together. Our fragrant pink rose becomes Grandmother's mashed potatoes in Christmas of 1972 except that we're watching the sea fifteen years later. Though the symbols may have spatial and temporal characteristics, we know it doesn't "make sense," as it does in waking life, to say that one event arose as the result of another event, or that a given object was a "logical" precursor of the next. The only way we can make sense of dreams is to view them as psychological realities with space-time attributes that are but symbols for basic underlying significances in our lives.

Significance is purely and simply a matter of focus. Whatever we focus upon is by definition significant, and whatever is significant is "real." To consciousness focused within the inner world, there is no difference between significance and reality. The terms are interchangeable. To consciousness focused outward, it seems that reality is material and significance nonmaterial, but in truth they are inextricably related. Anything of significance (that is, anything we notice or single out) is real; anything real (which we perceive with our physical senses) is also significant.

As we select a focus and form a significance, we create a reality for ourselves. A basic reality/significance for us in space-time is the feeling of being one self. Focused on this significance, we experience the reality of a certain body within a given time period and location, drawing to us events that resonate with the one self significance, and that serve to expand and change our idea of the one self. And within this gestalt of consciousness, choosing to focus on and thus identify itself as one self, is a myriad of lesser gestalts focused on lesser significances, all of which "add up to" the one-self reality. All of us to some degree are consciously aware of these "smaller" parts of ourselves. We consider them "us"—not a separate entity, but a part of our identity.

On the other hand, for the most part we fail to recognize that in turn we are part of a "larger" identity, an identity whose focus includes myriad selves like us, and whose experience and range of significance is proportionately greater. From this entity's perspective, the one self we focus on is but a part of its identity. Just as we nourish and support (and perhaps sometimes rail against, but always with an intimate sense of connection) those parts of ourselves, so too does the entity that includes us encourage and do what it can to help and inspire us, with the same absorption and concern. The more we can expand and stretch our concepts of personhood, the more we can accept and incorporate the experience and wisdom of this conglomerate being. Dreams are a primary means of doing so. The one self reality we so strongly focus in on in space-time fades away as we find ourselves appearing in many forms, still as "us" but a larger and more flexible us than our official waking self. And we go behind the scenes to see the larger significances from which we select those to real-ize physically.

The most important fact about significances, in terms of understanding them and ourselves, is that they involve *feeling*. In order for the meaning of something to be understood, we have to feel it. Our intellect puts two and two together for us, our feelings say, Aha, it's four! Without that aha, two and two equals four is meaningless. Once, when teaching first grade, I had a student who couldn't grasp the concept of counting. I'd line up five objects in front of her, count them off one by one, and then ask her to do the same. "One, two, three, four, five," she'd repeat, while her fingers worked at a different rhythm. In this case, she had the words but not the music, the numbers without the ahas. Many times Seth compares feelings to music (as in the feeling-tones exercise in the first chapter), talks of the deep chord of our being, of the hum of desire, of the harmonic rhythm underlying matter. This deeply felt meaning, striking us like a chord, is significance.

Symbols are significances manifested, and as such represent feelings. They are the ahas of meaning realized. The thoughts we think, the objects we see-smell-feel, music, our emotions—these are symbols of significances, of who and what we are: pure energized consciousness.

In space-time terms, of course, we say that symbols stand for "things," whether the thing be a chair, an event, or a state of mind. We think it's all pretty clear, what a symbol is and what's the real thing. But then we find that, depending on what we're talking about, anything can be either a symbol or "real." Is a democracy as real as, say, a flag, and what does "country" mean? Aren't the events of a wedding as symbolic as they are real? When it comes down to it, the reality of any phenomenon depends on our point of view. Even within space-time, our sense of reality fluctuates with our focus.

Seth makes a distinction between emotions and feelings. Feelings are deep underlying sensations unique to each of us, the essence of our significance, the expression of our identity, the song of our energy made physical. Sometimes, but by no means always, when we pick up on someone's "vibes," it is this energy we sense. However, if what we pick up on is in any way unpleasant to us, it has to be emotions we're experiencing. Emotions are feelings *with beliefs attached,* and the beliefs create the judgment: "unpleasant." Feelings just are, transcending any beliefs or judgments.

Feelings are always harmonious, like the rhythm section of a band.

Emotions, on the other hand, have many guises, like the lead guitar, as they reflect our beliefs about reality at any given time. Insofar as our beliefs are positive, our emotions will be positive, and vice versa: Negative emotions always symbolize negative beliefs. As such they are a powerful tool to use in discovering areas of significance we may not consciously have realized we were involved in.

Because of our tendency to focus waking consciousness on the sensual rather than the psychological, we are often unaware of our emotions and thus miss out on a good opportunity to learn about ourselves. Which is yet another reason dreams are so valuable, with their often raw (not to mention downright raunchy) emotions on display as in our dreaming mode we playfully try out various scenarios and get immediate feedback, discovering our deepest secrets, beliefs we would never admit to our waking selves, emotions we repress.

Every book on dreaming I've seen is based on the premise that the key to understanding dreams is understanding their symbolism. Luckily the trend is away from the Freudian notion that every symbol encountered in dreams, no matter by whom, has a set "translation" that we have only to look up in order to understand what we dream. Still, the assumption continues to be that dreams are symbolic and "reality" is not. To understand dreams we must concretize them, make them real, apply them to physical experience. It's a one-way street.

I'm not saying this approach is without merit, but only that it wouldn't work—if the assumption behind it were correct. If one world were symbolic and the other real, there'd be *no way* one could be translated into the other. In order for the two worlds to understand one another, they have to share a common experience that transcends the "reality" of either world. We see this with languages. There'd be no way one language could be translated into another were it not for the common experience (of, for example, a chair) underlying the words/symbols of each language. Translation is *always* a two-way street.

In the case of languages, though, all are more or less equivalent in that they are symbolization systems based on the shared experience of space-time. Spanish and English are equivalent in that they translate back and forth this shared experience. But dream reality and space-time reality cannot be compared in this way. It is more meaningful to say that material reality is a double translation and dream reality a single translation. Space-time is a translation of dream reality, which is in turn a translation of the world of dancing energy Seth has termed "Framework 2." Because that dancing energy is a basic experience shared by all "parts" of the psyche, a translation from one "level" of consciousness to another is possible, but before it can be symbolized in three dimensions, it must undergo an intermediate stage of symbolization, the dream state. In that sense, the waking state is less "real" than the dream state. The more "concrete" the symbols, the less they represent the dancing energy of All That Is.

A rose is a rose is a rose. Or *is* it? Basically we understand that the material objects we see and touch and smell are more meaningful than our sensory experience alone can reveal. And what they mean (how we feel about them) is a clue to, if not the essence of, our dreams. Certainly discovering the underlying significance of dream symbols helps us to understand why we created and continue to create our own particular material reality. But so too does an understanding of our material symbols help us to understand the rich world of dreams. It's a two-way street.

Exercise #12

Though dream reality is not organized in the same way the sensory reality of space-time is, it *is* organized, and that organization is more familiar to us than we think. Or I should say, as familiar to us as we think. And we think all the time. Everything we experience in the material world—taste, touch, smell, hearing, seeing—we think and have feelings about and thus experience in the nonmaterial world as well. And since those thoughts and feelings are not composed of matter with the accompanying space-time constraints, they are free to roam all over the place, so to speak. But they don't. They associate. They get together with other similar thoughts and feelings from other times and places, hang out together, compare notes, and make their own sense of this strange space-time reality they are so intimately involved with.

Psychologists call it free association, but free does not mean chaotic. Our thoughts and feelings have their own system of organization, and that system, according to Seth, is much the same as the system dreams follow, in which feelings (felt meanings, significances) take precedence and determine the events of the dream. We associate one event with other events (or objects or thoughts) because it evokes a similar feeling, an aha, a sense of fitting in, of adding to meaning in a certain area. Whether or not we are aware of making these associations, of course, we will continue doing so, because that's the way our minds work. But if we can bring to conscious awareness this associative process, we will be in a better position to make sense of our dreams.

Sit down with paper and pencil. Think of an important event in the past. Write down enough words to identify it. Relive that event as best you can, getting into the feeling of it, and once you do, let the associations flow. Write down the images that come, whether other events, people, objects, random thoughts. Be aware when you start going off the track, when your feelings have shifted. Stop writing.

Now look at what you have written and see if you understand why you have associated these events with one another. How do you feel about all of them? What do they mean to you? What have you learned from them? What beliefs and expectations about material reality do they reveal?

Exercise #13

Whenever you are aware of a strong feeling in yourself, let your associations flow, evoking past events, people, images. Then look back at what you have come up with and see if you can pinpoint a shared significance in all the examples. Look at what you are learning from them and at the beliefs and expectations revealed.

Exercise #14

Seth talks about the *circular* nature of dreams. Attuned as we are to the linear one-event-after-another experience of the senses, dreams seem chaotic. The events rarely spin themselves out to a logical conclusion. Often there is no discernible cause-effect relationship between an event that goes before and an event that follows. It could just as easily be the other way around. Past, present, and future seem to be interchangeable. Often an event will be interrupted by something entirely different and then take up where it left off. Or it will be repeated with variations.

Here is an example from one of my dreams.

August 13, 1988

I meet J and he is tall now, and I am glad to see him but somehow cannot talk to him here. It's as if I have to offer him help?/money? so the others won't know or they'll get it. I am in a car and come into a large rotary. I see J in a truck coming in, too. Instead of going where I am "supposed to" go, I maneuver the car in amongst the other cars and come up alongside him.

"We" are moving, and where we're moving is to the Cobb house, only it is in Hawaii and the house I moved from is not. D and P are going with me for they've never seen the Cobb house. I take a plane over from the old house and arrive at the new and there is P, who says she's brought some furniture for me. I remember I haven't finished doing what I had to do at the other house. Left lots of things there. I think I'm going to have to buy another round-trip ticket, but then I'm back at the house and the floor is being scrubbed and waxed by L and others.

Then I meet J. Is it the first time or the second? Did I dream this first and not remember it that way?

The reason for this circularity (notice the "rotary" in the dream) is that dreams are ordered around significances. In analyzing the above dream I could see that the events, disjointed as they seemed, mostly related to my feelings about helping and accepting help. That was their significance to me. I associated the event with J with other events—a slightly different theme on the same subject—which then reevoked J.

I think we can find the same circularity in waking life when we look for it. Since we create space-time out of the events of our dreams, and since those events cluster around significances, referring back and forth to one another in circular fashion, and for that matter, since our waking thoughts and feelings have the same circular organization, it only makes sense that the linear organization of waking life, which we pay so much attention to, only obscures the underlying order-by-association of dreams but does not supersede it.

There are a couple of reasons (other than our focus) why this circular order is not more evident. One is that we are dealing with many areas of significance at once, making the relationships among physical events less obvious. The other is that, unlike in dreams, where freed of space and time constraints a number of alternatives can be spun off instantaneously, in physical reality it takes time for all of these events to occur and objects to take their place. In the exercises above, you no doubt covered a large time period in making your associations.

However, I do think that at different times in our life we focus with more intensity on some significances than we do on others, and that if we know what these are we can see how events, objects, people, and thoughts associated with them keep coming up.

Think back on the last week and quickly jot down the events, objects, people, thoughts, and feelings that stand out. Whatever comes to mind about the previous week, write it down.

Starting with the first item on your list, see if you can find other items on the list you associate with this. Be sure you're listening to your feelings and not your intellect, which will want to categorize the items in some "logical" space-time way. Which items have a similar felt meaning to you?

Once you have grouped the items, try to come up with a name for each category that is descriptive of its significance, its felt meaning. Are there one or two categories about which your feelings are stronger than the others? If so, choose one of these; if not, choose one at random.

Trace the occurrence of this significance back as far as you can by associating the events on the list with ones in the past. Do you notice an increase or decrease? Some other pattern? What beliefs are involved with these events? Are the beliefs stronger or weaker now than before? What predictions can you make from all this?

Exercise #15

Everything we experience in space-time is symbolic. Actions, thoughts, objects, bodies, emotions—all are symbols of an underlying psychological reality. To the extent that we remember and study our dreams, to the extent that we learn the meaning (both waking and sleeping) of our own particular bank of symbols, to that extent we will understand what our psyche is telling us, where we come from, who we are.

Any physical event is but a small part of its nonphysical counterpart, one aspect we've chosen to focus on. For, given our space-time constraints and the nature of physical reality, we can never experience the entire event at one "time." We'll come back to it time and again, ever attracted to its significance, sampling more bits of it and adding to our understanding. This is what Seth means by circularity. But it is physically impossible for one person in one lifetime ever to experience a psychological event in its entirety. It takes a multitude of selves (reincarnational selves, probable selves) to thoroughly explore any event.

Seth talks of the "thickness" of a nonphysical event as compared to a physical one. A nonphysical event is not what we think of as an event at all but more like a central core of meaning out of which spring in all directions every possible interpretation of that meaning, in every possible mode (actions, thoughts, objects), each interpretation interacting with and changing every other, like an electromagnetic field. Every event in space-time, then, not only symbolizes the psychological reality from which it is derived but also implies a vast multitude of other happenings, whether alternate actions in the present, past occurrences, or future incidents. We have much to learn about our beliefs and why we make the choices we do by looking at the alternatives we did not choose or have not chosen.

Start with a simple event such as a routine trip to the supermarket. Think of the action as highly symbolic. What does it stand for or mean? Think of the events leading up to it as part of the event itself. Change some of them in your imagination and see how that affects your action. Think of the likely outcome of your action. What if you hadn't taken this action? What if you had gone to a different store or bought different items? What are a number of other ways you could have explored this meaning, other actions you could have taken that would have had similar meaning?

Think of other trips to the supermarket and how they differed from this one. Think of all the people at the supermarket and their different ways of shopping. Think of the ways people a thousand years ago got their food, drink, or whatever. Think of how they will a thousand years in the future.

Get in the habit of viewing your every action and every aspect of your reality as symbols standing for and representing a much larger arena of action from which you choose what you want to manifest according to your beliefs about yourself and reality. See your dream activity as an exploration of the many choices you have every instant of your existence.

Exercise #16

Stop right now and look around your environment for about ten seconds. Now, without looking back out at it, make a list of everything that you remember noticing. Don't list anything you now remember as being in the room or wherever you are if you didn't specifically focus in on it during those ten seconds.

Now ask yourself why you noticed what you did. What significance does each item on your list have for you? What feelings and events do you associate it with?

Ask yourself the meaning of some of the objects that you didn't take note of in that ten seconds. Why didn't you focus in on them this time?

Try this exercise when you're in an entirely different environment and compare notes. What symbols keep coming up for you in various forms at different times, in different places? These represent strong significances for you.

Exercise #17

After each item, write the first answer that comes to mind. What color is:

1. Happiness	_____	26. Gratitude	_____
2. Danger	_____	27. Warmth	_____
3. Summer	_____	28. Laughter	_____
4. Anger	_____	29. Hate	_____
5. Hope	_____	30. Your birthday	_____
6. Sickness	_____	31. Greed	_____
7. Harmony	_____	32. Friendliness	_____
8. Excitement	_____	33. Contempt	_____
9. Pain	_____	34. Goodness	_____
10. Love	_____	35. Courage	_____
11. Comfort	_____	36. Innocence	_____
12. Deception	_____	37. Joy	_____
13. Tenderness	_____	38. Fanaticism	_____
14. Wealth	_____	39. Democracy	_____
15. Fear	_____	40. Prejudice	_____
16. Jealousy	_____	41. Femininity	_____
17. Patience	_____	42. Work	_____
18. Desire	_____	43. Your favorite	_____
19. Devotion	_____	44. Freedom	_____
20. Death	_____	45. Marriage	_____
21. Masculinity	_____	46. Responsibility	_____
22. Loneliness	_____	47. Winter	_____
23. Hunger	_____	48. Imprisonment	_____
24. Sex	_____	49. Intelligence	_____
25. Pride	_____	50. Confusion	_____

In waking life we tend to associate colors with objects, viewing them as attributes of things we see, with no meaning of their own. If someone says the word "sky," we immediately picture blue. If "green," we think of grass. When asked to come up with what colors *mean* to us, of what they symbolize, though, we can usually come up with a number of answers.

White and black are perhaps the most common symbols in the Western world of good and evil, truth and deception. Blue means sadness and also masculinity, red is associated with rage, embarrassment, the vitality of blood pumping through the body. Green is newness, envy, or lack of experience, gold is equated with riches. We talk of cool colors and warm colors, of loud ones and quiet, of soothing and vibrant. These are a few examples of commonly accepted meanings of colors. In addition we each have our own personal meanings. But for the most part, because of our habit of associating colors with objects, we're seldom aware of how much color colors their meaning.

In dreams, though, the situation is different. An object ordinarily a certain color in space-time may be an entirely different, "unreal" color in dreams. It stands out, we notice it, realizing there's got to be a "message" for us. While red may mean heat, passion, strong feeling, blood, or life to the majority of people, perhaps it has an entirely different meaning to us. This difference in personal meaning applies to all colors.

The purpose of this exercise has been to get you thinking about the associations you make with colors. In the above list if you used the same color in relation to several qualities, group the qualities together (as disparate as they may seem) and see if you can find a central core of significance that applies to them all. Feel the meaning and then associate it with events in your life.

On a small notepad, write down your everyday responses to color in your environment: which ones stand out and how they feel to you. Begin to notice the colors that surround and form the background to the colors you focused on. See these as part of the gestalt, as part of the event of observing your favored color. Try to imagine how your perception would change if these background colors were not there. Or, if they existed but the main color did not.

Take note of the colors you experience in your dreams and see if your waking perceptions match your dreaming ones. What were the feelings accompanying the color in the dream? If these feelings are different from those you associate with the color in waking life, think it over. It could be that there's a hidden belief involved, and what you *think* is not what you truly believe. For instance, in waking life you may associate pink with babies and softness and tenderness, delicacy, femininity, gentleness and yet in dreams encounter pink as menacing and distasteful. This would be a valuable clue to a belief or cluster of beliefs you're not aware of.

Exercise #18

Seth has said that our habits are highly symbolic, serving as valuable clues to ingrained, often hidden beliefs—the stronger the habit, the stronger the beliefs. Through examining our everyday habits we can bring to light areas of significance we may not have noticed because they are such a part of our lives, so "factual," that it never occurs to us we have chosen that reality. Not that habits are necessarily detrimental; in fact I'd say most of them are helpful. But if we want to better know ourselves, looking at our habits is a good way to accomplish this. And if we have areas of frustration and conflict in our lives (and who doesn't?), by looking at our habits we can come to understand why. We can come to see areas of significance around which we have limiting beliefs and thus create an unnecessarily limiting reality.

List all of your daily habits, including cleaning (self and environment), foods you choose over others, common pastimes, security measures, words most often used in greeting people, TV programs and newspaper sections you're habituated to, thoughts that recur.

Examine the habits one by one, evoking the feelings that go with them. Use the feelings as clues to your beliefs. Any feelings you register as negative may lead to beliefs you find difficult to accept. (And vice versa, of course. You may be pleasantly surprised to find you have strong affirmative beliefs in an area you hadn't put much thought to before.) Somehow it is easier for us to notice and accept our negative *feelings* than it is to notice and accept our negative *beliefs*. I think this is because we see emotions as something that "just happen" to us. They're not our fault. But to *believe* negative things—well, we should know better. We feel guilty and down on ourselves, compounding the negativity.

Take particular note of habits you feel "neutral" about, neither good nor bad, perhaps "blah." This may be an area of conflicting beliefs, beliefs canceling one another out so that there is no forward motion, no growth and change, perpetuating the issue in your life.

Ask your dreams to help you with beliefs you want to change. Before going to sleep at night decide you will focus in on an area of significance you're having trouble with—a habit you're not happy with. Ask for a clear picture of your beliefs and for other perspectives and different beliefs. Trust your dreams to bring in new material, new ideas, new ways of viewing the significance. When writing down the dream the next day, record your emotions especially. Use them as a weathervane of your beliefs in that area. Also, in waking life focus your awareness on the habit that gave you your original information.

Merely observe yourself and feel yourself as you engage in the habit. Don't try to change it—the observation itself will change it. Over time, through the cooperation of your waking and your dreaming consciousness, the habit and/or the negative emotions associated with it will dissolve.

Exercise #19

Seth calls our skills "selections of significance." We're born with our own personal bank of symbols and a set of propensities, inherited from previous lives (in our terms). These operate as a latent "account" from which we can draw anytime. He uses languages as an example. If we're reborn in the same country we'll learn the language more quickly. Babies think in the language of a previous life before they learn their new one. We have many abilities like this awaiting activation. Some, like sight, are basic to the human species. When we open our eyes for the first time we activate internal visual symbols that serve as learning mechanisms. We cannot use our eyes properly until exterior images conform with the inner blueprint.

Some abilities are unique to us or to a small percentage of humans, and for this reason we don't take them for granted, as we do seeing, walking, and talking. It may never occur to us we have the inbuilt ability to sing beautifully, for example, or to excel at mountain climbing. More often, though, when young we play with our talents, then pick up beliefs from adults—that the ability is not useful, that one is highly unlikely to succeed at such an endeavor, that one should be pursuing something more popular—leading us to give up on it, to lose our concentration. The ability never has the opportunity to develop and mature.

Except, perhaps, in our dreams. In the dream laboratory we often test unused abilities, seeing ourselves "disguised." Onstage, a great concert violinist; in a garden, surrounded by gorgeous flowers; on a boat, sailing solo around the world; at work, finding solutions to difficult challenges. Often we hear people say, "It was only a dream." But how about those who "had a dream"—and followed it?

This exercise is in four parts.

1. If you have been writing down your dreams, great. If not, perhaps you can recall some recent ones. In any case, look to characters and incidents in your dreams dramatizing an ability, where problems were solved, skills developed, talents matured. Whoever the characters were in the dream, symbolically they represent you, and the skills your latent propensities, lying in wait for your actualization. Simply an awareness of these abilities in yourself can be enough to begin their activation. All it will then take is practice. It is up to you.

2. Think back to your childhood and to some talents you played with then—those you have continued to develop, those you have dropped. When I was eight, I wrote a play with a girlfriend, which we performed twice for our neighborhood friends, complete with entr'acte skits and organ music, a re-

tractable curtain (between living room and dining room), and costumes. I had forgotten about this until recently, when on whim I took a screenplay-writing class and in three months wrote two scripts, discovering I was a natural at it. The purpose here is simply to become more aware of your latent and not so latent propensities, to realize every action you take is but one facet of a multidimensional event you can draw from again and again. Or not.

3. The term "dream" is often used to mean "not possible now." "I dream of doing that someday" translates as "I know what I want to do is impossible now but perhaps someday it won't be." The trouble with this kind of thinking is that you aren't practicing whatever it is. Even if what you want does not involve a skill per se, it does involve beliefs and their accompanying emotions. You learn to be contented or feel powerful or whatever it is by being that way; by experiencing how a belief in contentment or power feels. With this in mind, look at some of the "dreams" you presently have. Each of these symbolizes a latent propensity you can start developing now—if you want to.

4. Our skills are our "selections of significance." Take a look at your present skills from that perspective. How do you feel about them? What is their significance to you? Why did you develop these particular skills and not some others you may have discovered in doing this exercise? What predictions can you make based on your present inventory of developed skills?

Exercise #20

We experience some events peripherally, some directly. A dramatic example is that of a plane crash. Not only do those in the airplane experience the event, but their relatives and friends do also, as well as those who see the plane go down, those who read about the accident or see it on TV, those who dream of it (either before or after the event), those who have fleeting thoughts of a plane crash, and so on.

We can tell the strength of a significance to us by how directly it involves us. We may know a lot of AIDS patients but not be one, ourselves. Or we may often hear of people who sighted UFOs, without our friends or ourselves ever having sighted one. In all cases the "proximity" of significances is constantly changing, with some getting "nearer," others farther away.

In this exercise, take note of your "peripheral" significances—events/symbols/objects you are not directly involved with but that are in your awareness to some degree. Gauge the degree of each and ask yourself whether its felt meaning is one you are thoroughly familiar with. Perhaps you have directly experienced this significance. Or perhaps you are being attracted to a new significance, or are curious about it. Ask yourself whether you want to put more focus on this particular significance or if you instead choose to focus elsewhere. You choose events through your concentration on them, so decide to focus on those events you truly want to see real-ized.

Exercise #21

For items below that describe a feeling, name an object, entity, or event you associate with it. For items that name objects, entities, or events, indicate a feeling that comes to mind.

1. A balloon	_____	35. Being photographed	_____
2. Rapture	_____	36. Horror	_____
3. Graduation	_____	37. Fireworks	_____
4. Running	_____	38. Living alone	_____
5. Sadness	_____	39. Alcoholics Anonymous	_____
6. Confidence	_____	40. Paris	_____
7. A headache	_____	41. Tenderness	_____
8. The sea	_____	42. Curiosity	_____
9. Fear	_____	43. Cooking	_____
10. Chocolate cake	_____	44. Listening to music	_____
11. War	_____	45. Lawyers	_____
12. Longing	_____	46. The World Series	_____
13. Rabbits	_____	47. Soaking in the tub	_____
14. The shopping mall	_____	48. New shoes	_____
15. Teachers	_____	49. Trust	_____
16. Pleasure	_____	50. Cheating	_____
17. Camels	_____	51. Dogs	_____
18. Divorce	_____	52. A bicycle	_____
19. The President	_____	53. Fascination	_____
20. Getting the wrong number	_____	54. Your mate/lover	_____
21. Mashed potatoes	_____	55. Peace	_____
22. Valentine's Day	_____	56. Vegetables	_____
23. Guilt	_____	57. Apathy	_____
24. A new car	_____	58. Blacks	_____
25. Animosity	_____	59. Concern	_____
26. An upset stomach	_____	60. Mother	_____
27. Russians	_____	61. Mountains	_____
28. An elephant	_____	62. Gays	_____
29. Excitement	_____	63. Smoking	_____
30. Dancing	_____	64. Embarrassment	_____
31. Secretaries	_____	65. Constipation	_____
32. Impatience	_____	66. Sisters	_____
33. Bandages	_____	67. A backache	_____
34. Going to the movies	_____	68. Getting paid	_____
		69. Fondness	_____

70. Wolves	_____	86. A thick steak	_____
71. Teenagers	_____	87. Shortness of breath	_____
72. A sore throat	_____	88. Insecurity	_____
73. Gaining weight	_____	89. Coming in last	_____
74. Baldness	_____	90. A cat	_____
75. Contentment	_____	91. Marilyn Monroe	_____
76. The Rolling Stones	_____	92. Boredom	_____
77. Colombia	_____	93. Hope	_____
78. Roses	_____	94. Changing jobs	_____
79. Tea	_____	95. Gaiety	_____
80. An eagle	_____	96. Senior citizens	_____
81. Wearing glasses	_____	97. Drawing	_____
82. Losing a bet	_____	98. Drugs	_____
83. Clouds	_____	99. Swimming	_____
84. An itch	_____	100. A scar	_____
85. Writing letters	_____		

Which of the above items did you have strong emotional responses to? What are the beliefs behind them?

Exercise #22

Once again, write a waking dream. This time begin with a strong area of significance for you. Focus on the feeling of it and then write your dream.

Afterward, examine the symbols you used. Change them into colors, feelings, entities, objects.

4

Photography as Metaphor

A remembered dream is a product of several things, but often it is your conscious interpretation of events that initially may have been quite different from your memory of them. To that extent the dream that you remember is a snapshot of a larger event, taken by your conscious mind.

Unknown Reality I, p. 206.

I've found Seth's photography metaphor so useful that I decided to devote an entire chapter to this topic. Not only does it apply to the process and products of dream recall but also to the way memory and belief systems intertwine in waking life.

Not a picture taker myself, I've observed a number of approaches to photography. One person I know uses his camera only on trips, getting strangers to take pictures of him as he tries to blend in with the foreign environment. Another is too camera shy to let anyone take a picture of her, but loves to snap candid shots of her friends. And then there are the camera artists who won't take pictures unless the light is just right and the composition just so. When they get their developed slides back, the content of the pictures may interest them less than the technical quality. I've known people who take out their cameras only to document special occasions, others who carry them everywhere, just in case.

Many approaches, but one I've never seen is picture taking at random, for no purpose—snapping for snapping's sake. The most avant-garde artist, seeking "realism," "naturalism," or "serendipity," using roll after roll of film in minutes, will still, with each picture, be making a choice, a split-second decision, as to which point in time, which image at which angle to focus on, out of the hundreds of thousands of split seconds, images, and angles. And because of this, no matter how "accidental" it seems, every photo will in some way reflect the worldview of its creator.

The same can be said of dream recall and waking memory: What we remember is purposeful, not random, and reflects our worldview at the time of the "take." From hundreds of thousands of images, the waking self chooses certain ones to recall and not others—the ones that stand out at the time, the ones most meaningful in the present.

But doesn't our analogy break down here? Doesn't the fact that photography captures images as they are happening in the present while memory recaptures images as they happened in the past make comparison of photography and memory impossible? After all, photos tell the truth—what really happened. Memory, as we all know, is often faulty. Take the classic example of two witnesses at a murder trial having entirely different recall of what happened. Photos would have told the truth.

Or would they? No photo is "true to life." If we accepted, for the moment, the idea that there is a purely objective reality "out there," existing apart from our subjective perception of it, even in those terms, no photo would be true to life. Because the nature of life, its very essence, is motion, no still photograph, not even a movie (which, after all, is a series of still photographs) could duplicate in its entirety what the direct experiencing of life's motion is, even, again, if we ruled out the subjective factor. Artists of photography recognize this—else they'd be painters instead. Their purpose is not to copy life but to encapsulate it, to capture in each never-to-be-duplicated instant an image that is suggestive of much more than it shows. A "frozen eternity" that nonetheless evokes life in its blooming, buzzing confusion. Except, the blooming, buzzing confusion is itself a myth.

Rarely do we experience life as confusing; for the most part it makes sense—its own sense to each of us. Seth says we would think it miraculous how all the individual consciousnesses participating within space-time manage to coordinate their efforts and keep the system operating if we knew how very few similarities of perception they have to go on. How very few similarities and how very many differences. He is referring not only to differences among species or life forms, but to differences even between two very intimate humans. We think of our sensory perceptions as being more accurate than our psychological ones, and yet Seth says even the position of objects in space is slightly different to each conscious entity. Telepathically we agree on an approximate location and let it go at that.

What this means is that "objective reality" is an approximation arrived at as the result of an unspoken agreement among entities, and as such is a subjective, "artificial" construct. Two photographers taking pictures of the "same" reality are photographing their own space-time approximations of a felt significance. And those viewing the photographs will see *their* approximations. From this perspective, snapshots are a direct analog to memories and dreams.

Still, what *about* the fact that photographs are direct, a recording of an event as it originally happened, while memories are indirect, a recording of an event as remembered? Since this is the case, how can the two be compared? Wouldn't our photographs of an event differ from our later memory of it? If asked to remember the event without the photographs before us, wouldn't we come up with very different images? And also, if somehow, magically, the same event were to happen now, wouldn't we choose to take different photographs from before because we are different now than we were then?

But the point is, all perception, all reality creating, all life, takes place in the present. Whatever we perceive now is a reflection of who we are now. Looking at photographs of a "past" event is a present event, and our perceptions in viewing that photo will reflect our present worldview. Looking at the same photographs tomorrow when today is in the past, our feelings and perceptions will have changed. If asked to remember a photographed event without the photos before us, we might very well come up with entirely different images, but then, on viewing the photos, find that they agree with and validate our "memories." As we've already seen, what we perceive as the past has its own existence in the present and it changes to stay in harmony with our perception of the present and the future. Thus, were the same photographed event magically to happen now, of course it would be perceived differently, and so would be a different event. The pictures we took of it this time would be different. However, were we to compare the pictures taken of it the first time around and those taken the second time around they would harmonize and support each other in reflecting our present point of view.

On a wall near my desk I have "randomly" arranged a collage of photos that never fails to be a main attraction for visitors. I myself never tire of looking at it. Some photos I'll merely glance at, others I'll give a prolonged study. Sometimes I get up from my desk to look closely at a detail I hadn't before noticed. What strikes me is how much I *interpret* each image, how much my memory, expectations, and feelings are involved in what I see, and, especially, how much my present outlook influences the context. One day a picture may have a relaxed feel to it and the next day, a nervous quality, reflecting my emotional state at the moment. We all do this; we all assign a context to photos we view, a context melding with our present experience. What would someone else's impression be, I wonder, of that picture on the wall of my daughter, then eight, petting a tiny white lamb on a Moroccan roadside, with sheep grazing in the foreground and a djellabah-clad shepherd looking on. Or someone else's view of this picture of my favorite married couple, smiling out at us, arm in arm, he with his neck in a brace. No doubt the pictures have much different meanings to other viewers than they do to me.

When I meet someone I've previously seen a photo of I'm usually surprised at how he or she looks in real life. Photos of my friends "look like them," since what I see in the picture I automatically put in context with my known experience of them. The picture merely stimulates my memory of them as a living, moving being, and that is what I see. How I feel about a given friend on a given day will make a difference in what I see, and sometimes will bring some surprises, but for the most part the photo conjures up my flesh-and-blood friend. When I see photos of strangers, I also provide a context for them based on my experiences with other people, but when I meet the unique being, I'm usually in for a surprise.

Something else that strikes me about these photos is how they harmonize with one another in a way I can feel if not always articulate. Here I am at eight with a girlfriend, and then at sixteen with a boyfriend, and then as a young mother with my small son. There I am growing and changing, with family, friends and locations revolving about me. It's interesting how many sites have water in them—rivers, lakes, especially ocean beaches, and how many of them are in foreign climes. Interesting too that out of all the photos, not one is of a husband, not one of the university ambience once an integral part of my life, not one, for that matter, of my days as a college student. And why, I wonder, did I choose to put the picture of my parents on the porch of their cozy little home in that particular spot with those particular pictures around it? I really can't say, but I sense its rightness there. Taken as a whole, the collage represents my self image, what is of significance to me, what I believe life to be all about . . . for now.

Seth likens dream recall to the process of photography. The conscious mind, casting about amidst the blooming, buzzing confusion of subjective events called a dream (for dreams often are confusing to the waking self tuned in to linear cause-effect reality), chooses but a few images to focus in on and to "remember" in waking reality as pictures, as "snapshots" the waking self can then fit into the context of his or her belief system. Just as the real-life photographer's choice of image for any given photo is not a random one, but motivated out of a felt (if not clearly understood) purpose, so the dream photographer's choice is not random, but fits with an overall purpose not always obvious but always in keeping with his or her belief system about the nature of reality.

Seth says that many of these dream "photographs" are pictures of events we want physically materialized—some of which we do decide to use in space-time eventually, as we saw in the chapter on precognition. From that perspective, the dreams are blueprints for the later snapshots we take and hang on our walls. It could be that every snapshot we take was already taken "before," in our dreams. And that the motivation for putting on film one particular image as opposed to any other image comes out of our dream experience: We're simply following our blueprint.

Exercise #23

Find an old photo of yourself. According to Seth, that past version of yourself exists now. Study the photo with this in mind. In your imagination become that being as he or she exists now at the age in the photo. Provide a detailed three-dimensional environment and, as your character, move about in it, interact with others, go about living your life, feeling your feelings. Let this earlier you become aware of the you of now, of what he or she is becoming. Stay with this feeling as long as possible.

Then leave the scene, leave the photo, come back to "here."

Look again at the photo, but this time imagine it emerging from the dream dimension, from a dream snapshot taken earlier. The image you see before you is one you first saw in your dreams, and took a snapshot of, a dream snapshot of a probable reality that you later chose to actualize.

Imagine now the other dream snapshots you took at the same time, in your constant revision of a blueprint to follow in creating space-time reality. One by one, imagine the other versions of you in the many other dream snapshots of the blueprint—probable selves all of them, probable versions of each other in their similarity of beliefs, each unique in his or her choice of direction at this point in time. Imagine these probable selves existing today, having followed a different path in a reality you chose not to materialize, having their own dream snapshots, their own blueprints.

Exercise #24

Now find a more recent photo of yourself. Experience this earlier self as you did in the previous exercise. Be that age now, be that person.

After you come back to yourself, reflect on the difference in feeling you had with the first version and the second. What beliefs predominated in your experience with the first photo? What was especially significant to you about him or her? In your experience with the second photo, what was most significant and what were your beliefs in this area?

Exercise #25

Find a photo of yourself socializing with others. In your imagination, relive the occasion in its fluid motion of events, people, and objects. What is your predominant feeling during this occasion? What is its main significance to you? What meaning are you exploring?

Return your attention to the photo. See it and feel it as a frozen instant that encapsulates the emotions and significance of that remembered occasion. Sense its origin in the dream world, one of a series of encapsulated instances to choose from in creating your reality. Understand and feel the significance of this simple photo.

Get in the habit of looking at photos both from a sensory and a psychological perspective. Let them bring to you not only the sights, sounds, and smells of the occasion but also the psychological reality underlying them—your worldview. Realize that no matter when the photo was taken, it is a statement now, about your beliefs and attitudes now. Your sensory and psychological responses to it are clues to your current beliefs.

Exercise #26

Go through your old photographs and make a pile of those you want to use in a collage—pictures you've taken, pictures others have taken, any subject, any time period. Even picture postcards. Use your intuition to guide you in choosing the ones that feel significant to you.

Spread the selected pictures out so you can see them all. Look them over, feel yourself gravitate toward this one or that one, choose the one you feel most drawn toward. Staple or tack it on the wall, or paste it on a large piece of cardboard. If you find you have a plan in mind—"I'll put all of these in this area, all of those in another" or "most important in the middle, less important toward the outside"—let go of it. Feel dreamy as you do this, letting the images come out at you and spontaneously take their places on the wall.

Once the collage is finished, view it as the visual embodiment of your psyche, which you can explore in a number of ways.

1. Examine every picture in it, whatever the subject matter, with the idea that it symbolizes an entire gestalt of thoughts, feelings, beliefs, and significances within yourself. In my collage is an ancient Italian woman soberly absorbed in her creation of delicate lace, one tiny thread at a time. I could spend hours with this image alone, exploring the significance of the person as a past self, as the personification of patience, persistence, and skill, or as a symbol of beliefs about aging or womanhood. The lace itself has meaning on a number of levels.

2. Take note of the pictures you put close to one another. They have a connected meaning within your psyche. Sense the significance of each picture, then shift your focus to include the two or three or four pictures grouped together. What connections do you sense?

3. Take note of the pictures far apart. What are their significances? Can you sense their distinctness, their separateness in significance? Do you sense any conflict?

4. Notice the colors. There may be a predominance of certain colors, or color and mood may seem to match. What is significant about the colors in your collage?

5. Take a look at the proportions of pictures in these categories as a clue to beliefs about yourself and the world. Others may occur to you as you go down this list.

   a. What proportion of the pictures are of you?
   b. Of these, is a larger proportion from one given time period as

opposed to others, or are they evenly spaced throughout eras of your life? Or, are they all recent? All old?

c. What proportion of the people in the photos are of the same sex and what proportion of the opposite sex?

d. What proportion are group pictures (three or more) as opposed to pictures of two or of one?

e. What proportion are of family as compared to friends? Parents as compared to children?

f. What proportion are close-ups? Middle distance? Long shots?

g. What proportion are taken in or near your home? Far away from your home?

h. Posed shots versus unposed?

i. Outdoor versus indoor?

j. Country versus city?

6. Notice what is *not* in the collage. Earlier I mentioned my collage had no pictures of my previous husbands or of my university ambience, both important symbols and space-time entities in my life at one time. Although of course it is obvious to me here and now that I am not married and have not been for a long time and that I am no longer at the university or in any formal "job," it still came as an aha when I noticed I had "unconsciously" omitted pictures on those topics from the collage. Those old symbols are just not "me" anymore in the way that some old symbols still are. This doesn't mean I'm no longer attracted to the significances once symbolized by husband or by the university setting, but that those symbols have been replaced by others as I explore the same essence through other forms.

7. From time to time, make changes in the collage to reflect changes in you.

Exercise #27

Before going to sleep at night, tell yourself you're going to take photographs of your dreams, and that you will be aware of doing this while you are dreaming. Take with you an excellent camera that automatically snaps a picture whenever you see a dream image you want captured on film. All you need to do is think "snap" and the camera snaps. With this kind of equipment you are sure to bring back an interesting batch of photographs. Tell yourself the pictures will be the first images you see in the morning.

Seth says some people may wake up with a clear picture instantly in mind while to others it may come later in the day. If you don't have an image on awakening, then be alert for images occurring later. The more you practice, the better the results. Even if you regularly remember your dreams without the aid of an imaginary camera, try this exercise. It will enhance both the quality and quantity of recall.

For each image that comes, write a thorough description. Include how you felt during the dream and how you feel as you're recording it. What beliefs does it reveal? How does the image fit into your present waking reality? Each picture gives you a small glimpse of the reality underlying space-time, and together they acquaint you with the choices you have ahead of time, so to speak, so that when the situation arises you will be prepared to make the choices you like best.

Exercise #28

Most of us can remember the past to some extent without the need of an imaginary camera to capture our images for us. But, as is the case with dreams, using the imaginary camera technique will enhance both the quality and quantity of recall.

Decide you'll take a photographic expedition into the past with the same think/snap camera you use for dreams. If you want, use a photograph as a point of entry into your past, beginning your exploration there and letting it take you wherever your associations lead, snapping pictures as you go.

When back from your journey to the past, write a description of each picture as you did in the exercise above. Keep in mind that whatever you remember and record of your past is a reflection of your present beliefs. If on this excursion into the past you met an earlier you who believed he or she was, say, unfairly treated, realize this is a belief of yours now. It may seem to be a belief you have outgrown, but if you had truly outgrown it, you would not meet it in the past, for the past self and the future self change to reflect the changes of the present self. Whatever beliefs you hold now, your past and future selves hold as well. You are the one in charge.

Exercise #29

Try a waking dream using the imaginary camera. This time, rather than writing it down as it's happening, go into the waking dream state with a camera and take pictures. Afterward write down and describe the images. Compare the imagery of your regular dream with that of your waking dream and also with the memory images of the last exercise. You will probably find them different in a manner that is difficult to describe. That is because they arose out of three different states of consciousness, three different ways of observing.

5

Interpreting Dreams

Your dreaming experience . . . gives you a guideline that will help you understand
the nature of your own psyche, and the deeper reality in which it has its being.

                                            The Nature of the Psyche, p. 32.

One day the receptionist at my dentist's office briefly described to me her
dream of the night before and asked me to tell her its meaning. The same day
an acquaintance asked me if I'd read Freud on the interpretation of dreams.

What a "coincidence." I'd just that morning been thinking about how I'd
approach this chapter, anticipating a lot of people's expectations about dream
books or dream classes. One expectation is that someone else can tell you what
your own dream means (the receptionist's notion), and another is that this can
be done because the symbols of dreams have a universal meaning (my acquaintance's notion, via Freud). And now, here were these people "just happening"
to voice those thoughts for me so I could see them out there in space-time.

The next day someone else voiced yet another expectation I'd been
thinking about, and the gist of it is this: Since the primary purpose of
dreams—at least from the viewpoint of the ego—is to give us specific
directions on how to deal with daily life, then learning to interpret our dreams
better will lead to a better run life. Now, I have no argument with such a
result. While it is certainly true that we cannot expect others to interpret our
dreams for us or for symbols to have universal meanings, it's also true that we
can expect our dreams to give us guidance in our everyday lives. What I do find
arguable is the assumption that the main purpose of dreams for us as space-
time beings is daily life guidance.

Before the previous summer, I had spasmodically remembered and written down my dreams, but never until then so extensively and with such
intensity. All of a sudden here I was night after night having dream after
dream. I often spent most of the next day writing down and analyzing them.
Consciously I hadn't decided I was going to make dream recall and interpretation an important part of my daily life. On the other hand I had long wanted to
write a Seth workbook on dreams (and was urged to by fans) but felt I did not
have enough experience with my own dreams to do so. Now the experience was
happening.

In thinking back to when the dreams started coming, I realize what I
wanted from them at that time—and therefore what I focused on—was a
deeper understanding of my psyche, my inner self, my roots. In waking life I

had worked a lot with my beliefs, using techniques from my two previous workbooks to uncover them, change them, create new ones. I'd made a lot of progress and I'd reached a plateau. It seemed to me I'd gone as far as I consciously could with this, and the only way I could make more progress was to expand my consciousness, to go deeper, to explore parts of my psyche that had not yet been revealed to me through the work I'd done. I saw dreams as serving this purpose, and so, that is the purpose they served for me.

It was not until I decided to do this book and began rereading (for at least the tenth time) all of the Seth works, and after I'd read many other books on dreams, that I discovered the purpose I had chosen for myself "just happened" to be the purpose Seth emphasizes. (What makes the Seth material so unendingly provocative for me is how full of surprises it always is—almost as if the ideas are newly created just as I'm ready to focus on them.)

Seth has very little to say about the use of dreams specifically to solve life's problems. He does mention such a use but makes no suggestions and gives no exercises or procedures in that regard. He has a bit more to say about "out-of-body experiences" (another focus of popular interest with dreamers), especially in his early work, but leaves it to Jane Roberts and Sue Watkins to fill out that topic. He also talks to some extent about precognition, as we have seen, but from the perspective that precognitive dreams (and successful predictions) clue us in to areas of significance within us, and therein lies their value. He has similar comments to make about nightmares, saying they are of value in bringing to light material buried deep within.

Indeed, the vast majority of Seth material on dreams takes the perspective that dreams, for us in space-time, are a remarkable guide to the psyche because they are a meeting ground for the "conscious" and the "unconscious." He says we are at a point in our development where we're ready to "come awake" in space-time, to expand our usual waking consciousness and widen our focus. This requires becoming more conscious in the dream state and more "dreamlike" in the waking state. There are various ways of accomplishing this, and he proposes a number of exercises toward that end.

Not to say that the "solution to life's problems" approach and the "expansion of consciousness through deeper self-knowledge" approach are mutually exclusive. The solutions we find through dreams come out of insights into our deeper nature, while deeper self-knowledge enables us to make wise decisions for ourselves in space-time. It's just that the former approach limits its focus to "relevant" meaning within the psyche, getting to know the forest tree by tree, while the latter focuses on inner dynamics so as to know the forest and thus its trees. Solutions take care of themselves.

A number of books on dreams stress the value of group work, a value lying not in other people's interpreting our dreams for us, and not in learning what symbols "really do" mean, but in the fact that as a part of group work everyone has a number of dreams to interpret—their own and others'. In working with other people's dreams, viewing them as if they were their own, group members gain new insights and perspectives they might not have gained working strictly with their own dreams.

This makes sense. Just as we experience space-time from our own unique perspective and remember our past according to our beliefs in the present, so too we experience other people's dreams in that way, interpreting them in that way. But an added bonus in working with groups is that our interpretation will in many ways stand in contrast with other interpretations, giving us a clear look at our worldview and belief system, and a broader perspective on reality. To use an example from teaching, I had a number of foreign students in my classes who, through having lived in the United States and experienced a different culture, had gained an entirely different perspective on their own culture. They hadn't noticed a number of aspects of their culture until they came over here and recognized the absence of those aspects, or saw them viewed differently. Many of the beliefs underlying their culture were invisible to them because that culture was the only one around.

We can get this same perspective on our dreams through group work. If we interpret a dream (either our own or someone else's) mainly in sexual terms, and someone else in the group sees it in a different light, as a dream about creativity, while another associates it with death fears, our sexual orientation, because it stands in contrast with the other orientations, may be noticeable to us for the first time. We come to understand that "reality" arises out of us, reflecting inner meaning and beliefs.

For that reason I've decided to present some of my dreams for you to interpret in your own way, as if you had dreamed them. Following that will be a section with my interpretations. Through comparing your interpretations with mine you may get self-insights otherwise hidden from view. Because my dreams were motivated out of a desire to better understand my inner dynamics, the messages in them for me pertain more to that than to specific happenings in space-time, though of course the inner and the outer are inextricably related. If your main desire is to deal with waking concerns, then I am sure these dreams will have pertinent messages in that regard. Because of the multidimensionality of dreams, they can be interpreted on a number of levels by each individual.

For that matter, the meaning of dreams changes with time. If we go back a long time later and read a dream we've recorded, we'll see it in a new light, getting new messages from it, sometimes in addition to the old messages, sometimes in replacement of them—much as we do with photos. Any dream, no matter when it occurred, will in some way address itself to our present beliefs and worldview. One of the rewards we get for record keeping is a widened perspective, watching our psyche as it goes through its changes.

In analyzing the following dreams, here are some questions you might ask yourself.

1. What for you was the underlying feeling tone of the dream—gloomy, frenetic, bubbly, intense, funny, or . . . ?
2. Do you recall having a similar feeling recently in space-time?
3. What does the dream seem to be about?
4. What do various people, actions and objects in the dream symbolize, represent, mean to you?
5. What associations can you make to these?
6. What is the message of the dream? Or, what did you learn about yourself? About your beliefs?

Please write your own interpretation of a dream before you read my interpretation in the next section.

I have changed the names of my personal friends who appear in these dreams to protect their privacy. In any case, the dreams aren't really about those people, but about aspects of myself represented by them.

Exercise #30

Audrey's Speeding Ticket (7/10/88)

Audrey gets a speeding ticket while driving my car. I am with her. We go home and wait for the cops to come and arrest her. They do and she is handcuffed, but then there is much discussion, and the police leave after telling me Audrey said I am the one who should take the rap since it was my car and my trip. This amazes me. One lady cop says she thinks Audrey is schizo.

Then we are at Peter's place and I seem to have a date with his older brother, who is depressed and lies around. Other people are there who have already eaten a fancy meal, one of the items being skewered meat, but there isn't anything left but potatoes and gravy, which I eat in the dismal atmosphere.

Audrey and I are waiting for a ride (hitchhiking), and I say good-bye to the brother who just lies there and doesn't respond.

Exercise #31

Anthrax (7/19/88)

We are all involved in some sort of joint enterprise—several men plus my daughter and I. Chaos reigns, nothing is getting done. I say to Tony, who is in charge, that it would probably be best if I just went elsewhere and got out of the way. He, to my surprise, says emphatically, "No, not with all there is to do!" and so I ask, "Well, what can I do?" He says, "It's about time to top those plants."

He points to some plants growing in a row with seed pods at the top, some of them already having opened enough to reveal a few fuzzy spores (like dandelions). I go to the plants and reach down, and just as Tony is yelling, "NO!" I remove the pod from one plant. Somehow I throw it or it goes up in the air and bursts, and a cloud of spores comes down to earth.

"Anthrax!!" says Tony. "That's anthrax. You have to leave town immediately, be under quarantine."

Everyone is being careful not to have the spores touch them. But I have been touched, and so has my daughter. They tell me something about it being microscopic and growing. I ask if anything can be done. "No, just get away."

Then ensues a frustrating segment where my daughter and I are trying to get out of there but feel immobilized, and I wake up.

Exercise #32

Drunk at a Restaurant (7/22/88)

I'm with my daughter and we go to a restaurant and I am drunk. All of a sudden I don't have any clothes on. The waitress and owner, a black couple, say, "Take your name tag off." Somehow, though I'm naked, I have a strap with a name tag on it. I wrap myself in a towel. I really want to talk to the owner, to explain my behavior, but I don't have the chance because people keep coming into the restaurant.

Exercise #33

Traveling Through Europe in a VW Camper (7/23/88)

Bob and Tom and I are traveling through Europe in a VW camper. Tom is doing all the driving. One night he pulls over to the side and water is boiling in the radiator. It boils and boils. I look out the window and see the radiator cap is off and the water is bubbling up and over from a seemingly endless supply. We get out and notice that the camper's rust-infested body (it had been freshly painted previously) is falling apart. In the front it is totally ravaged, the left headlight having fallen out. The sides still have some painted areas left, but I wonder whether the camper can make it from here, our first destination, to the next two we're supposed to reach.

Next thing I remember is, I've somehow lost them. The camper has gone off without me. But then Bob shows up. I'm glad I'm not alone. We circle the town, walking, hoping to meet up with Tom in the camper—trying to figure out where he'd be waiting. Finally we do spot him and he is looking upset and presents me with a note, which says his spirits are low, there is no plan when to leave, where to go. I say, "Yes it is a good idea to have a plan." I decide to get Bob to figure it out. He likes to do that kind of thing.

Exercise #34

I Meet Jane Roberts (7/29/88)

I come to a party with others to meet Jane Roberts. I get a glimpse of her when her car drives up—she's in the backseat. Dark eyes. Not sad-looking, but, well, not of this world. She has with her a library book with a protective plastic cover and two pairs of glasses—reading glasses of graduated strength. She is then engulfed in a coterie of admirers.

I feel relaxed and happy and natural. I think I should introduce myself to her, tell her I wrote *Create Your Own Reality* and tell her about the new book, but she seems to have gone. Then someone says, No, "she" is here. And I look down a row of seated people to see a short, very dark man. I call to "her" and address her as her and he says, Call us "us."

He is very personable and is quite taken with me. Finally he excuses himself from the group and says, with good humor, "I have fallen in love with Nancy Ashley," and he takes my arm and escorts me off, down some stairs to a group of small rooms at the bottom of the house. I feel very good with him. I'm aware that two or three other people are about as he takes me into this one room but doesn't close the door. What I'd had some inkling of is about to happen. He wants to make love!

I hesitate a bit because of the nearby people. At this point he is wearing a colorful elephant costume. "Oh let's" or some such he says cheerfully as he begins to take off his clothes. I too begin to take off my clothes. I remember thinking, He probably misses physical sex. Then he asks me some questions and gives me some information. We are in an embrace when I am aware of people looking in and going off titillated. He is perfectly at ease.

Then I'm back upstairs and I find Jane's book and two pairs of glasses and think she must still be here or she'll be back for them.

Exercise #35

Hawaiian Mafia (8/9/88)

I am a captive of the Hawaiian mafia. I somehow escape and am recaptured. I've gone against the mafia so I should be in for punishment. The leader takes me off. I am not afraid. He is warm and gentle.

Exercise #36

End of the World (8/10/88)

The end of the world is imminent. A natural holocaust has been proved to be coming very soon, in hours. One of "us" (a tripartite entity) elects to stay "down below"—in the lowlands, where it is dark. "I" am going to meet my end up higher. The third part stays with "me." I am prepared for this ending of life, and calm. The emotional tone of all this is flat. The color dull gold comes to mind. We wait for the fatal moment, it passes. And we wait some more. We and others around us (and now the landscape seems like Switzerland) begin to stir, to begin cautiously to suggest it's not going to happen. We begin to move about, visit with others. The world comes back to life.

Exercise #37

I Find a Baby Elephant (8/25/88)

I find a baby elephant and bring it home. We—Mary and I—have fun with this cute little guy. At one time I am going to give him a bath. I start cleaning out his ears, which are remarkably open and smooth, but I keep finding more and more sand. Can never get it all out. I decide to wash only the ears, and when I start doing it I find one spot on the outside, which I scrub and scrub but cannot get clean. I finally give up but Mary still wants to give the elephant a full bath. However right now there's no room in the kitchen sink.

Now Mary and I are making love with a Chinese guy (who I think the elephant turned into) and it seems to me we had trouble getting him off, but this part is hazy. He and his wife have emigrated from China because he is out of work—he was a congressman and she a journalist.

I am lying with him and I ask him how tall he is. He seems startled and says he doesn't know. I say, "You're this much taller than I" (indicating with my fingers) "so you're five five." He says, "I think I'm the shortest man I've ever seen." "No," I say, "a lot of people from other countries are short as compared to us."

I go into the other room. I want to cook dinner. There is a group of people watching TV. A show about dolphins? So I go back in the other room. Now there are people sitting around and this little kid who used to be the elephant and the Chinese is hitting at the red-painted wall with a stick. To stop him from doing this I take this thing I have in my hand, which is a stick with several points on one end, like a mace. And I touch this to his face. He immediately reacts extremely to it. It appears to be very very ticklish. He finally rolls on the floor almost in a faint. Someone else in the room tries this on his own face with his own "tool" and says, "Wow, is that ever ticklish." It is intoxicating just to watch their reactions.

Exercise #38

The Second Room (8/31/88)

I have moved into a cottage. Someone I knew had it before and I'd seen it, but when I look at it to rent this time I see only one of the two rooms. I fix it up, move in, into the one room. It has a balcony around three sides, narrow, from the railings of which I hang curtains.

Friends, including Barbara, come to visit. Barbara of course does her thing of disrupting everything. One man describes the place as "stuffed." I hadn't thought so. But now it seems as if there's a different rug and is there a couch? Well, it keeps shifting before my eyes.

After they leave I straighten up and it is then that I walk into the other room. It is a while before I realize it is part of my place and that I've seen it before.

It is much larger than the first room, with high ceilings and a huge window looking out to a spectacular view of the sea with an offshore island that rises in golden splendor, and in the foreground the waves lapping on a beach (some distance away) with a hill sloping down to it from here. This room is more private than the other (which opens out to the center of a compound)—it opens out to trees. These are the stunted gnarly kind such as you see around Carmel.

In the room is a warm potbellied stove, a parrot in a cage, a dugout area with brown grass in front of the view window, where I think a couch looking out could go.

The floor looks to be dark parquet wood, but on closer examination it is tile. An ancient john composed of two rooms is off to one side of the entrance. A pull-chain toilet is in one room and a washbowl in the large other room, which is overgrown with weeds.

Can't remember a kitchen in either room.

The furnishings were Salvation Army–style—early hippie modern, only not colorful.

Exercise #39

The Bottomless River (9/8/88)

I live on a farm. I write to a group of Christian Scientists and they come to visit me en masse. One of the women—young—and I really hit it off, and she tells me (and as she does, I'm there) of an old village on a bottomless river. This is a mystery and so is kept from the general public. But the people in the town know the legends about the river, and they swim in it, gaining access through openings in a concrete platform that they keep covered so the kids won't fall in.

This next part has to do with a hose, music, and my book (on dreams). Somehow we have this music belonging to an evil man, which we want to play while running the hose. This is essential to the writing and development of my book. But if he hears it being played he will demand something—money, I guess—or take the hose away. I get a glimpse of him—he looks ordinary but with an every-now-and-again flash of blackness from his eyes.

One of the men tries playing the music/hose and has to stop when the evil man's gang comes by. Then I try, hook it up, and it plays and waters and no one comes by, and I think, *Why this tune, why not Mozart? It would do the job as well.* At one point the evil one comes by (when the music is not going) and now he has the audacity to have an evil face drawn on his T-shirt—which seems particularly malevolent to an elderly farmer.

Exercise #40

Married to Paul (9/12/88)

I am married to Paul. His wife seems to approve. I seem to feel that he needs my help. Early on he voices one of his outrageous opinions about people and I tell him I won't have him being so unfair. Later, talking to my mother (who has said, "If I were you, I'd stick with it no matter what") I tell her about this—the idea is I will not tolerate everything. Paul says, "You'll have to change, I won't."

One of the trials of the marriage is that I must somehow "go way down deep"—it is a necessity.

At one point Paul and I have traveled somewhere and we're feeling good together. We see land way to the south and he says, "Let's drive there." And I say, "It's got to be a thousand miles. We can't get there tonight." And we check and find out that, sure enough, it is that far.

So I must regularly "go deep deep down," and it is very enervating/ exhausting. Takes all of my strength/power. But I must, no question about it. It seems to be space travel within to unknown places. Others go with me to help but I am the motivating force, the energy that takes us there. I remember during one "trip" we had to stop over at some stage and then go on to another and another. Three stages. When I am doing this, I feel so very deeply deeply concentrated, and my mouth opens wide.

Exercise #41

Reading and Wandering (9/16/88)

I am with others in a North Shore house. It is all cluttered and curtained, not at all open and airy as it was when I lived there. Some man is going to read to us, so we all lie down and listen. He goes on and on. I "wake up" in the dream to find him still, still reading. He goes on reading all night long. I am very tired, though I did sleep through a lot of it. I ask him if others slept. "A lot of them did," he says. He just wanted to keep reading. I feel very well treated that someone would be that caring.

I am at a conference and I see Mary. She tells me that in my reading I mixed up the adjectives and adverbs, and that I couldn't get the verbs. People repeated it three times. Impatient. All that noise and confusion.

Then I'm at this seaside area where I'd been before, near where we're staying. Suddenly a café and dressing rooms, etc., materialize there. It is a standard model (portable?) unit found in this area at other seaside spots. I am glad it is there because the place needs it. The nice beach below needs facilities. I think it is here that I see Mary and she tells me of the reading.

Then I am going to where we're staying—Jane Hanson's apartment in an ornate hotel-looking building—with brass and marble lions, etc., sculptures in front. Her apartment is on the bottom floor left and "we" come in through the glass doors. Jane is asleep on the couch, which is of ornate brass.

Jill Hanson, her daughter, and someone else are there and they also comment on my reading. I am now in a very bad mood, feel very tired and very stubborn and ornery and misunderstood and insecure. I say that I have heard enough about my reading (which I think was a sort of dream interpretation where people were telling me what they thought and I wrote it down). I tell them that if it had been a good reading then I'd like to be complimented; if not, to be quiet.

I am in a foul mood. I want comforting, but am not willing to ask for it or to soften—bristly and keeping people away. I say I'm going, hoping they'll protest. They don't and I go off through the back of the apartment and through an area that looks like a Beverly Hills furniture shop. They do not follow and I want to go back, but cannot find the way.

A gang of very young men, partying, spot me, and want me to join them, and I hesitate—mostly because I'm thinking, *They couldn't possibly be interested in me; I'm too old.* But I end up wandering around with them and feeling better. Especially nice is a blond young man.

I spy Mary, who is dressed in a smashing dress, flowing, off the shoulder, loosely held together. She is on the other side of a partition and I call to her. She comes up, sees the men, and hesitates. I say, "Come, let's have coffee," or some such. In order for her to get there she has to backtrack and go up one short flight of stairs and down another. She finally joins us and is "with" a young, dark-haired man.

I am now feeling good and also trying to find my way back to Jane's. The blond man wants me to come stay with him and I say something like, Well, it (our relationship) could never be serious (because of the age difference). Then I see him in clear bright light, and he is about my age. This encourages me.

My Interpretations

Audrey's Speeding Ticket (Exercise #30)

This dream revolves around my ambivalent beliefs pertaining to "rationality" and "irrationality." To be irrational (Audrey in the dream) is to be crazy and thus not responsible for one's behavior. On the other hand, to be rational and mature (the older brother) is to be depressed and immobilized.

The "I" in this dream (as in many of my dreams) is partly observer and partly participant. In the first "act" she participates (playing the rational role), seeing how it feels to be the responsible one (car owner)—the unjustness of it all that Audrey should "blame" her, that she should think it was her "rap" when she wasn't the one doing the speeding. Her amazement at this attitude is tinged with envy that Audrey can "get away with" something and she can't. Someone has to be in charge, call the shots, and since Audrey's craziness (unpredictability?) makes her ineligible, "I" am elected. But it's a burden.

And it is with this burdened feeling that Act Two begins. (The feeling/significance attracted the events/symbols.) Here "I" is more of an observer exploring further what rationality means. It is associated with men, as is often the case in our society. Men (such as the brother) are rational and women (such as Audrey) are intuitive—and therefore irrational. And it is associated with maturity (the brother is "older"). These added dimensions add more weight to the burden, and the brother, carrying them, lies around depressed, immobilized, unwilling or unable to respond. And "I" am supposed to have a date (be mated, paired up, identified) with him!

The other people who are there represent hangers-on, more irresponsible ones getting a free ride (fancy meal). And they have eaten all the meat, which represents substance and meaning (but skewered on sticks by the rational mind). What is left for "me" to partake of is mashed potatoes and gravy, and it is dull, depressing, unsatisfying fare. Nothing nourishing here.

And now another switch, to Act Three, where I'm paired up with Audrey once again and we're going hitchhiking. Neither one of us is going to do the driving, take all the responsibility. I can take leave of this image of gloom and powerlessness.

MESSAGE: The rational part of me, realizing how unrewarding, unnourishing, and stultifying it is to "be in charge," is ready to let go of the belief that it has to be the driver (or be responsible, if not), and, teamed up with the irrational, be open to the unexpected (hitch a ride).

Anthrax (Exercise #31)

Unlike most of my dreams of the summer of 1988, this one I could hook up with a couple of specific incidents in waking life. One of them was a confrontation with my daughter in which I vented more emotion than I had in years. The other was the reading of a book on the male and female within (the rational and intuitive/irrational once again), its thesis being that an inner integration occurs when the female is free to come up with ideas, and the male to carry them out. This made sense to me—or I made sense of it—in terms of what I knew about my inner dynamics at the time.

Chaos reigns within and nothing is getting done because the female (represented by "me" and my daughter) are waiting for ideas/instructions to come from the male. The male wants the help of the female, but the ideas must come from him. The plants represent the emotions in this dream, and the emotions (associated with femininity) must be nipped in the bud, topped, pruned back.

Instead, in an impulsive (intuitive) gesture by the female, the emotions are let fly (just as I had let them fly with my daughter a day or two before in waking life) to "infect" others—to infect the males, for the only females on the scene have already been infected.

When I looked up "anthrax," I found it meant "a carbuncle on cattle, caused by microscopic organisms, and contagious to man." Contagious to *man*. A disease originating with a different species (female as cattle?), contagious to the male species. And how does this disease manifest itself? Through a carbuncle, or boil, which inevitably must erupt, burst forth, just as the emotions do.

MESSAGE: This dream dramatizes conflicting beliefs and their resultant fears and hopes. An old belief is that if the emotions and intuitions are given free reign "something terrible will happen." And an emerging one (beginning to manifest itself in space-time as per the incident with my daughter) is that it is okay to act impulsively, to be emotional. After all, nothing terrible happens to me from having been "infected." But the "quarantine" (waiting period) suggests some caution. "Wait and see." I see the relationship of this dream to the previous one. This one complements the first and expands the meaning of rational, male, being in charge; both dreams show my readiness to do something different, or at least to entertain the notion.

Drunk at a Restaurant (Exercise #32)

My daughter represents the feminine, impulsive, emotional part of myself, and when she appears in dreams, "I" take on her characteristics.

Another dream dealing with (and expanding upon) fear of "losing control" (being drunk), totally vulnerable (naked and exposed) by bringing my emotions (self and daughter) out front, into public (a restaurant).

The black couple (the gloomy, no-nonsense, critical, proprietary and responsible service-to-others oriented part of myself) want nothing to do with this other side, don't want "me" identified (via the name tag) with them. "What will people say?"

MESSAGE: an emerging and ever more "out there" aspect of myself (the emotional/intuitive/feminine) feels vulnerable, wants understanding and acceptance. But the critical, dominant (rational/masculine) aspect continues to busy itself with other concerns (other people in the restaurant).

Traveling Through Europe in a VW Camper (Exercise #33)

Yet another dream about the rational and the emotional and who is in charge. (I had requested dreams dramatizing this sensed inner conflict, and I got them!)

In this dream, Tom represents the emotional, out of control aspect, and Bob, the rational. The VW represents my body. The dream is parallel to the first (Audrey's Speeding Ticket) in that the irrational is at the wheel leading to breakdown (à la getting the ticket), except that, here, the rational side has let go of feeling responsible or desiring control. The "I" in this dream is a new entity representing a growing cooperation between the two "sides."

The body has an endless supply of emotions though its heart (left headlight) is broken, ravaged by all of this inner conflict.

What are the three destinations? We're at the first one, and it is: breakdown. Where can we go from here but to healing? After that we'll be integrated, liberated from this struggle.

At one point, the emotional (female) side decides to go it alone but soon returns and asks for help. The go-between will give this job to the male, who is good at planning and instigating action.

MESSAGE: (I'd been having aches and other bodily symptoms for a few days before this dream.) The breakdown, painful as it is, nevertheless portends healing and integration. A new cooperative energy has been mobilized.

I Meet Jane Roberts (Exercise #34)

In this dream the "I" represents the ego, Jane Roberts the inner self (the mystical side, the seer, the soul), the dark man "us," a collective, a symbol of the unmanifest world in general, our source.

Jane brings a book and two pairs of reading glasses. If one doesn't work, the other will. She really wants me to learn and to see. The book and glasses appear again at the end of the dream. She and "they" really want me to notice.

Going off downstairs with the dark man—to a deeper level of relating, a deeper state of consciousness. My *self*-consciousness gets in the way a little bit here as I have fleeting thoughts of being "seen," known for who I am, even of being laughed at.

I loved the elephant costume in this dream, which to me represents the male role (the trunk a penis extraordinaire), which can be donned and doffed on whim. He puts on his male costume so he can have sex with me (in my female costume). But both costumes are soon removed since "having sex" at this level of consciousness is symbolic, a celebration of union, an initiation into wholeness, a joining with the source.

MESSAGE: Healing and integration are taking place within, I am getting in more conscious touch with that deep loving core of myself and have nothing to fear. I am supported and nourished, and I have the tools (glasses, book) for self-knowledge.

Hawaiian Mafia (Exercise #35)

The "I" here again is the ego, and the Hawaiian mafia the "underworld" I visited in the last dream. I see this short piece as a playful look at some interrelated, and for the most part outmoded, beliefs of mine. Here they are:

1. We are in danger of being controlled by dark inner forces (the irrational).
2. Therefore we must be rational. Being rational is being responsible.
3. "I" don't need any help. Being helped means being controlled.
4. An expansion of consciousness or "spiritual growth," as it is often termed, results in ego death, the supercession of the spiritual over the physical, the giving up of one's space-time personhood.
5. We will be punished for our sins, one way or the other.

In this dream I play with these ideas, but there is no sense of dread or gloom. It is like a charade. The mafia leader here is the elephant-costume character of the other dream, and I totally trust him.

A cat came to mind in association with this dream. (I identify a lot with cats.) You open a door to let a cat in or out, and it has been waiting to come in or go out, but will it go in or out? No, it waits awhile to show you its independence (however well the cat and you know it needs you). It must have its token rebellion, it must let you know it is its own person. That is the way the escape felt in this dream. "Just want you guys in there to know I am who I am and will do what I do. And I don't need any help from you."

This last idea is still with me to some extent, projected outward into space-time. But what is interesting about this dream is the trust, the giving over of the ego self to the "leader" without fear.

MESSAGE: This exploration through dreams has increased my feeling of inner support and love. The rebellious feeling I sometimes have is more playful than anything. And I'm increasingly more willing to trust the messages from my intuitions, to let myself be led.

End of the World (Exercise #36)

I see this dream as a dramatization of my fears/doubts about my growing sense of power (the underworld/Hawaiian mafia). That much power could annihilate everything (natural holocaust). The belief, again, that the ego will be overcome/superseded by the powerful deep self, that expansion of consciousness means loss of the familiar space-time self.

The tripartite entity here is the inner self/soul, which "stays below," and the body and ego, who, "above," experience the waiting and fearing—only to find out there is nothing to fear.

MESSAGE: Once again, fear not!

I Find a Baby Elephant (Exercise #37)

I spent most of a day analyzing this rich dream, viewing its symbols from many perspectives, filling ten notebook pages. It would take many more pages than that to explain here what I didn't need to write down for myself as I went through that process. So, instead, I'll make some general observations.

The baby elephant/diminutive Chinese man/little boy with a stick entity represents the sexual, sensual, intellectual, and spiritual in me, all layered together, inextricably related—essentially, a dream about the integration going on within (if in its beginning stages). The elephant image you'll recognize from a previous dream, and he represents here spirituality. Then he transforms into a Chinese (and my association was with Confucius, sagacity, the mental and intellectual), and then into a little boy with a stick, which I associated with the physical—the message being that the spiritual, mental, and physical are different aspects of the same thing. That each image is in some way immature reflects my present perspective.

Especially interesting to me in this dream is the nurturing female (both in her careful methodical guise as "me" and in her more adventurous mode as Mary—who wants to wash the whole elephant) and the "sensitive" male. These are personas I hadn't met before in dreams and I see them as emerging out of some new beliefs that are still a bit tenuous.

I see an affirmation, too, of the body and sensuality and touch, as per the "orgasm" at the end, which also represents the almost unbearable euphoria of direct spiritual contact.

MESSAGE: The present turmoil I'm experiencing (in waking life) is reflective of important (and positive) inner changes and realignment.

The Second Room (Exercise #38)

(These are verbatim notes from my journal, to give you an idea of what my analyses sometimes look like before editing.)

Okay, so there's a whole 'nother room there for me to discover—and I do discover it in the dream. The most interesting part is the view. The golden offshore island. Which, well, it was like STRAW—a big stack or arrangement of straw.

Straw into gold.

So, I'm moving into this whole new part of my psyche that has been there, is familiar to me, I have glimpsed it before, but now seems more accessible—I got a detailed look at it.

The previous room was very inward looking—don't remember any windows. Really a small room, not much space. Stuffed. Stuffy. Intellectual. Time to spread out.

This new one is MUCH more comfortable, spacious, pleasant than the other—though I am dissatisfied with the floors (fake) and the oldness and lack of pizazz. Is this the way I see myself? Well, lately maybe.

Ancient plumbing. The bathroom overgrown with weeds—from disuse? My body not used, sexually?

The dugout area in front of the window where I envision putting the couch—more groundwork has been done there than elsewhere, and it makes a view (into the future, into the gold possibilities, into the psyche, into the depths of the psyche) more accessible.

I am not satisfied with the floor—not real wood. Fake. I've covered over the true floor with a fake one—am I glossing things over? Or is it that I want to get to the bottom of things—and still haven't quite? Yes, that seems on.

Why California? Well, that is where a lot of the groundwork for all this was done.

First time I can remember a house dream with a view!! Yes! Thanks!!"

MESSAGE: The inner world is becoming ever more familiar to "me."

The Bottomless River (Exercise #39)

I see the farm as a communal live-work situation, something I continue to be drawn to. "We are all in this together." My introduction to metaphysics was through Christian Science when I was ten. So in this dream my sending for the Christian Scientists represents my desire for inner guidance.

I remember in the dream being a bit concerned about what the farmers' reactions would be to the Christian Scientists, afraid the Christian Science philosophy wouldn't be acceptable to them, and not wanting the Christian Scientists to proselytize.

The young woman I hit it off with—whose face was the only one I really saw in the dream—reminded me of someone I knew who had dropped out of the main*stream* to live by the Russian *River* and go deep within. In the dream she acts as my guide, telling me of a bottomless river, which at one point at least is underground with access to it covered up so that children (the innocent, unknowing) won't inadvertently be taken into the depths. The river, of course, is the so-called unconscious, the depths of the psyche. I remember feeling drawn to it in the dream. I saw the covered openings. Did I lift a cover and look in? I think that I did.

Meanwhile, back on the farm, the book is being grown, cultivated, and this is done through watering and music. Water, essential to life, the main substance of our bodies, refreshing, renewing, growth-producing in plants. My book is an organic thing that needs nourishment just as plants do. But not only physical nourishment; it needs spiritual sustenance as well, in the form of music. This is crucial in the dream, and there is some danger that it will be taken away, that it "belongs" to someone—that it is private and exclusive and not to be shared, not accessible.

The two parts of the dream, first the river, then the book, are closely related in meaning. Writing the book means going deep within, and there is some apprehension on "my" part. Not only because I know not what I might find there but also because someone or something is standing in the way.

I didn't know what to make of the evil man at first, until I decided to question him as part of my dream analysis. What came out was a fear of being taken as a proselytizer, or being proselytized myself. I'd felt this before even meeting the Christian Scientists, and feel it much more so when writing a book myself.

What the evil man says on questioning is that he wants "credit" for his ideas (the music). Without that they couldn't be used. To me, the idea that I, or someone else, has the truth and another person doesn't is at the heart of proselytizing, and in the dream it was obvious I considered this an evil. I certainly did not want to be taken for a proselytizer with "exclusive" ideas. The elderly farmer in the dream represented an aspect of me that is particularly suspicious of strangeness and fearful of proselytization.

Luckily the "I" of the dream recognizes that music, like truth, is universal. Everyone has it. "Why this tune, why not Mozart? It would do the job as well." Music is there for the listening/taking in, not someone's private property. And so, of course, is consciousness.

MESSAGE: This dream illustrates my fascination with the psyche and desire to go into its depths (which I've been doing). It also illustrates my fear of being a proselytizer, of presenting the material as if it were my invention, as if I had the power over others of taking it from them (and therefore depriving them of its nourishment) on whim. It shows my fear of being proselytized myself, too.

Married to Paul (Exercise #40)

A marriage of convenience between opposites, each of whom is equally stubborn and opinionated: "I won't have you being so unfair." "You'll have to change, I won't." Both are travelers. One travels on the surface, through space and time. The other travels below the surface, deep deep down.

MESSAGE: This dream tells of the growing cooperation of the female and male aspects of myself, who have given up none of their individuality (nor do they intend to) but who need and help each other in their travels. For both, traveling together means going further (deeper).

Reading and Wandering (Exercise #41)

Another long, rich dream that I spent a lot of time with, relating it to a number of present-day issues in my life, to old, outdated (but still operant) beliefs, to risk, to change.

The parts about readings—first the man at the house, later myself at a conference—had to do with my waking desire to get a dream group going, doubting my ability to carry it off, realizing it takes a lot of trust for people to open up and reveal a dream. In the dream, the man doing the reading goes on all night, putting most people to sleep. His intentions are good but he was (I found myself thinking as I wrote) "all words and no music." (Compare this to the Bottomless River dream.)

Then "I" meet Mary, my dear close friend who represents to me "the risky edge." And I meet her at a seaside resort (adventure), and it is in such an atmosphere, where people are playful rather than "serious," that I give a reading. The reading, I remembered as I was writing this down, consists of dreams of my own that they were supposed to interpret. I get the adjective and adverbs mixed up, and can't get the verbs right. And so they have to repeat everything and there is much impatience and noise.

A couple of beliefs are obvious here. One is that the only way to communicate, to be understood, is through words, but words don't work very well, and the other is that THIS IS SERIOUS BUSINESS (one that continues to appear to me in different guises). Because of both of them I am frustrated and go on to the next scene.

Jane and Jill Hanson represent to me my distant past. In fact, the Jane I knew in waking life has been dead thirty-five years. I go through this old-fashioned, ornate building to visit her and her daughter, who represent some beliefs of mine that were strong then (and still operate today to some extent), e.g., it is absolutely the worst thing in the world not to be understood, just as bad to be criticized, and I don't want to hear it. The ugly old feelings that went with the beliefs were strong and familiar. I make sure to perpetuate them by refusing comfort, by refusing to be understood, and come back (a bit reluctantly) to the present.

There I meet a gang of young men (my adventuresome, youthful, "non-serious" aspect—what Jung might call the animus) and, despite misgivings, go around with them. Soon Mary materializes, another (more "feminine") version of this risky, leading edge part of my personality. It is somewhat difficult for her and me to join forces. She has to go up, down, and around in consciousness to get together with that past-ridden character.

The ending is affirming as I come back into the present ready, tentatively at least, when allied with my "risky" self, to go right into "uncertainty" and the unknown—to give up "oldness" and "seriousness." I am pleasantly surprised as my vision clears, as my fears go away, and trust sets in.

MESSAGE: Don't get hung up on words; trust your feelings, trust yourself.

6

Playing with Dreams

You cannot begin to understand how you form the physical events of your lives unless you understand the connection between creativity, dreams, play, and those events that form your waking hours.

The Nature of the Psyche, p. 141.

We all are skilled artists whether or not we are aware of it, for we dream, and dreaming, says Seth, is the quintessential art form. Unlike space-time art, dreaming requires no physical or mental effort. It is "the mind's free play," a spontaneous, joyful activity in which the mental energy we don't use in waking life (and Seth says we could use much more than we do) goes into the creation of fantastic dramas, some shared, others private, all, despite their freedom and spontaneity, providing a framework from which we select the events we will later experience in waking life. But the "practical" function of dreaming is a side effect, for the mind dreams not in order to provide a training ground for event forming (though it does) but because it enjoys the activity, just as we enjoy those activities that follow our natural bent.

Seth often comments on how seriously we take everything here in space-time, when it is more natural to be playful. Children, not yet trained to be "serious," consciously create play dramas, sometimes scaring each other silly, trying out events in the world of their imagination, seeing how they look and feel, being at the same time the creator and the participant, realizing they can "switch channels" anytime. Adults rarely allow themselves such creative play, and though it continues to characterize their dream life, they may not be aware of their playful and creative heritage, viewing dreams as serious business indeed to be studied in a scholarly and detached manner, the artifacts of a foreign consciousness.

We tend to identify with and accept as official that portion of our consciousness that seriously and intently focuses on space-time and to view that portion of our consciousness we use in the dream state as belonging to someone else. Even as we accept intellectually the *idea* that we create our own reality, we still *believe* it is not "us" who does it, but that "other self" we have met in dreams. And we set off on our quest into the unknown with sober determination to get to know that other self better.

It's like a cat chasing its tail, in a way—though not nearly so playful and spontaneous. The cat gets so caught up in the chase that it doesn't experience itself as belonging to that tail, or the tail as belonging to it, or how it feels

85

being an entity with a tail. Similarly, in our serious quest we cannot possibly experience how that portion of our consciousness feels in its playful creativity. We observe it but don't identify with it. So long as we take such a stance we cannot possibly come to know ourselves as the multidimensional beings that we are.

The many exercises in this chapter (and elsewhere), then, are best approached not in the spirit of "I'm going to get to the bottom of this, by God," but rather that of "Let's see how it feels to spin off symbols this way, create images that way, following whim." In this chapter we'll look at many ways we can come to understand and become more conscious within dreams. In the next we'll look at ways to experience the consciousness we associate with the dreaming state while awake.

Exercise #42

Many so-called primitive cultures knew intuitively that symbols were just as "alive" as they were, that each symbol was quite literally an entity, a gestalt of energy with its own core of meaning and significance, its own attractive force. They understood the cumulative power, the positive energy for them of certain symbols, and, harvesting their dreams, chose these to incorporate into their art, music, rituals, and stories.

Of course we're constantly dealing with symbols in our culture (how could we escape it when space-time itself is a symbolic construct?), but seldom with the focused awareness of our forbears. We're scarcely conscious of how we're drawn to and influenced by the symbols we surround ourselves with, whether they appear to us in the form of clothing and cars, tasks and celebrations, or attitudes and feelings. Because of this we get mixed messages from symbols, feeling ourselves attracted first this way and then that, the healing power of one symbol canceled out by the negative influence of another, and we fail to take advantage of an energy we could use to mobilize ourselves in a positive direction.

While it is not necessary (and ultimately impossible) to articulate the underlying significance of a symbol, it is necessary and relatively easy to *feel* it and thus to determine whether we want to have more of that energy/attraction in our life. To paraphrase Seth, If it doesn't feel good, don't do it (or use it, or focus on it). And if it does, harness that energy!

The game in this exercise is to bring into waking reality those symbols you encountered and felt positive about in your dreams, knowing you are creating a space-time "field" around which events will form. One way is to draw or paint your image. This is a popular technique in Jungian analysis, and I have talked to people who've had amazing results, attracting events they knew to be connected in a meaningful way with the dream symbols they'd in various ways recreated in space-time.

In one of my dreams I had a clear image of a vivid pink and blue Saturnlike planet with rings around it. I painted this in acrylics and hung it at the foot of my bed. I couldn't say specifically what it meant to me except that it had to do with my inward search and that it felt right. After a few days I had another dream in which I saw the same image but with the rings melded together in a much tighter circle around the inner core. I changed my painting to reflect this. As time went on, the dream image and my space-time replica underwent more changes to the point where they bore little resemblance to the original but still elicited somewhat the same feeling (though the feeling did change with each change in image). As a word-oriented person I had never before with such conscious focus explored meaning in this fashion (though I very soon recognized that I had been doing this all along without noticing). Just this one experience got me in the habit of focusing on symbols, feeling them, and consciously making a decision whether or not I wanted to affirm them in my life.

There are of course many ways for you consciously to manifest dream symbols in space-time. You can sculpt them, create a song about them, dance to them, cut pictures out of a magazine, create collages, or buy toys or other manmade articles that to you represent replicas. It may turn out that your space-time manifestation does not at all resemble the dream image but feels right to you. Whatever you end up with, put it on display where you will see it frequently, get zapped by the feeling it elicits and so expand your unspoken understanding of that significance in your life, and recognize it as it appears in other forms around you in space-time.

Exercise #43

A friend I'll call Jon had a dream so memorable he still can describe it in vivid detail twelve years later. In the dream he saw on the mantelpiece of his living room a snaillike creature, seemingly of clay, which nevertheless came alive and slithered down onto the floor where it began devouring ants and other bugs, increasing its size as it did so. After a while this large "blob" (as he now saw it) was outside, absorbing into itself ever larger prey—cats, then small dogs. It was when the creature was about to engulf a German shepherd that Jon woke up in horror.

He was going to a therapist at the time and took this dream to his next session, where he came to understand in words what the blob represented to him: a heavily conservative, bigoted part of himself that "sucked up" all of his energy so that there was none left for the many creative endeavors he felt drawn toward. Obviously he strongly believed in the reality of this "obstacle" to his creativity, and met it in various guises in space-time. But this was the first time he had met it in such a concentrated feeling-fraught form, the first time he felt he had something "concrete" to deal with.

How he dealt with it was to make a detailed drawing of the blob, then, at the same time that he muttered an "incantation" composed of phrases he spontaneously summoned up; he drew flames around it and colored them bright fire red, adding more and more flames, and incanting more and more until a different energy took over and the energy of the blob faded out. He said this represented a turning point in his life, the point at which he felt born (or reborn) into creativity, as the activities of his life since then attest.

Every symbol we encounter in our dreams is of course there for a reason and of use to us. While "higher" consciousness makes no judgments, ego consciousness finds some symbols representative of positive space-time results, some representative of negative ones, depending on its belief system, its expectations, and its desires. In many cases, simply by "accentuating the positive" we can bring positive results into our lives. In others, however, when the negative feels very powerful, a transformative approach such as the one above can be very helpful in changing our understanding, our beliefs, and our waking experience.

Again, it is not necessary to put in words what the symbol represents to you (though verbally oriented types often find comfort in doing so) so long as you clearly feel its impact. It helps if you can look upon the symbol as a welcome learning opportunity rather than something to be feared (thus increasing the negative energy). And the more playful you feel, the more successful you'll be. Pretend you're once again a child playing "cops and robbers" or "the bogyman will get you." Treat the symbol like a plaything you can make into anything you want.

You might pretend your image is a balloon you can blow up and pop; that you have a magic wand to wave over it; that dousing it with water will melt it; that your musical sword will slay it; that out of its burning ashes will emerge a beautiful bird; that a kiss will rehabilitate it. You've seen how to do it in fairy tales, so now it's your turn to be the hero or heroine, and rid your world of that negative influence, creating a positive force in its stead.

Exercise #44

Another useful technique, both for uncovering the meaning of symbols and for transforming negative impact to positive, is dialoguing. Gestalt psychologists use this all the time. Its value hinges on how deeply we can identify with any given symbol, whether it appears as a person, object, or idea. The game is to become the symbol and explain yourself to other parts of the self, how you feel and why. I've always had good results doing this, discovering attitudes I was unaware of, resolving negative feelings. Often during the dialogue I found myself, in the imagined role of the symbol, changing in form and feelings.

The Bottomless River dream of mine (Exercise #39, last chapter) had an "evil man" character who claimed to own the music necessary for the writing of my book, and whose primary purpose was to thwart those of us at the farm who used the music. Though the "I" of the dream ends up carrying through on the cultivation despite this character, and comes to a felt sense of resolution within the dream, my waking self wanted to know what beliefs the man represented and why they aroused such fear and hatred, especially on the part of the "elderly farmer." So I staged a conversation between the evil man of the dream and the "I" character.

The gist of the resulting dialogue (which I didn't write down) is in the previous chapter. The key lines went something like this:

"I": Why won't you and your gang let us play the music?

MAN: It belongs to me; it's mine, not yours, will never be yours.

"I": I need it for the cultivation of my book.

MAN: Then you'll have to pay me for it.

"I": Pay you? How?

MAN: You must pay homage to me, give credit to me, admit it is mine, not yours, can never be yours.

In interpreting dreams it is important to stay with it until you get that aha of recognition, when you sense the meaning even if it cannot be fully expressed in words. For me, "pay homage" and "give credit" resonated within and brought to the surface several conflicting beliefs around the idea of proselytizing, discussed previously. The evil man faded away, having served his symbolic purpose in the dream.

In another dream I met a character named "solo soldier," whose problem was that he no longer had a job. Previously I had got in touch with a "fiercely independent" part of myself, accepting and befriending her, thus defusing much of her militance. In dialoguing with solo soldier, it came out that he represented this militant portion, an energy now thwarted. He needed something new to "fight for." I asked him to please welcome and support and give his strength to the nurturing female portion of my psyche, who had been given more "room" once the independent part had voluntarily disarmed. He agreed and took a new job title: cooperative spirit.

A procedure used in Gestalt groups is for each person to tell his or her dream and then to become, and speak as, every aspect of it. If a staircase was in the dream, the person speaks as the staircase: "I am the staircase. I am creaky and worn. People never use me anymore. I feel lonely." And so on. The more playfully you can approach this exercise, the better the results.

Dialoguing can be usefully combined with other techniques such as painting or performing a transforming ritual—whatever it takes to achieve a sense of resolution. This is an unmistakable gut-level response that automatically changes your perspective on the dream, changing you.

I found writing down the dialogue as it is going on to be disruptive, but you might want to make a tape of it.

Exercise #45

Until recently, my experience in working with dreams had been spasmodic. Most mornings I'd awake with a vague remembrance of dreaming, but only rarely did I attempt to write something down, much less analyze or interpret what I'd written. My resistance to dreaming was an expression of the belief "I haven't got the time."

But then as my desire to do a book on dreams grew, and along with it my willingness to spend time writing them down and thinking about them, my morning memory became more vivid, the dreams more accessible. Soon I found myself spending four or five hours a day in dream recording and analysis. It felt as if I were catching up after years of neglect.

However, after a while, though I continued to look forward eagerly to the unfolding of each dream, I also began to feel overwhelmed and frustrated because I was neglecting other activities I enjoyed. Obligingly, my dream memory began to fail at times. Some mornings I could remember nothing at all even though I knew I had dreamed and that in the dream I had told myself I would remember. Other times I could remember but a fragment or two, which I didn't write down, having the attitude that I had to fully remember a dream and fully interpret it, or forget about it, thus sabotaging myself via my Taurean intensity.

One morning I woke up knowing I'd had at last two long dreams, but couldn't remember them. I so wished to bring them into conscious awareness that I decided I would just write down whatever came to mind, even fragments. Disappointed, I could think of only four terms: "skin," "Caveat emptor," "Memphis," and "pumpkin." I would have given up at that point had I not been curious about the meaning of "Caveat emptor." I knew I'd seen the term before but couldn't remember what it meant. So I looked it up: "Let the buyer beware." I was intrigued; what could *that* possibly mean? And what, if anything, did it have to do with the other words, so different from one another? Why had I remembered those particular words out of all the material from that night's dreams? I decided I would see what I could do with this limited set of data.

First I wrote down in my journal the feelings and images I associated with each word.

> *Skin:* soft, cover, sensual, deep, scrape, remove, surface, stroke, caress, feel, love, thin, vulnerability, openness, sex, tan, sun. [I found it interesting how I veered away in my associations from deep and somewhat scary feelings back to space-time terms like "tan" and "sun."]

Caveat emptor: buyer beware, Latin, foreign, a warning, dishonesty, cheating.

Memphis: Tennessee, Joe [a person from Memphis whom I had recently had an unpleasant encounter with], a hick, foreignness, another world, not to be trusted.

Pumpkin: Cinderella, pie, roundness, fullness, ripeness, sweet, plump, cheerful, magic.

Hmmm. Well, definitely, each term meant more to me than before, but I still wasn't getting an aha. (Once that feeling of understanding comes and everything falls into place, it is hard to conceive of not having understood immediately, it seems so obvious.) At that point I decided to try a technique I'd taught my writing students to use in generating ideas for writing. It's called mind-mapping and its effectiveness is surprising, considering how simple it is to do. It consists of placing key words in balloons and connecting them, thus switching from a strictly linear ("left brain") perspective to a pictorial ("right brain") one.

This is what I came up with in my journal:

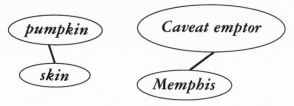

What I hadn't seen clearly before was that "skin" and "pumpkin" were closely related in the feelings and images they elicited, as were "caveat emptor" and "Memphis." So I paired the terms and put them in two circles side by side, like this:

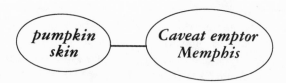

I then saw that the two paired terms beautifully symbolized my conflicting emotions and beliefs around what a friend of mine once described as "hanging it all out there for the world to pass on." Two situations in space-time came to mind, one having to do with a man a friend wanted me to meet, saying we would be ideal mates, and the other with my book *Create Your Own Happiness,* which I had just the week before received my author's copies of. Here is what I wrote in my journal:

Some anxiety here about presenting "self" to the outside world. The world of Joes and cheats. Hmmmm. So, it appears that I am projecting distrust. Who or what in me do I distrust? Buyer beware. Who is the buyer? What does she need to beware of? Getting cheated? Who's doing the cheating?

Am I afraid I'll cheat others, misrepresent myself?

If I am the buyer, what is it I'm buying that I need to beware of?

Let me see. How does this relate to recent events in my life? Aha! This has got to be about my upcoming meeting with this bloke D. Yes, that has certainly been on my mind. Hmmmmm. I'm disappointed that I am not "braver," but thanks for the insight anyway.

Come to think of it, this also has to do with *Create Your Own Happiness*. Well, *of course* it does! Why didn't I see that before? Here I was wondering whether the book *buyers* would take issue with some of the things I say in it. So, yes, of course. Thank you, thank you. I hadn't realized I felt as vulnerable as the dream shows me I do.

Four terms was all I remembered of a night's dreams, and yet from those four terms I was able to arrive at a message from which I learned things I hadn't consciously recognized about myself and my beliefs. And in the process I discovered I didn't have to have a full-fledged dream to get a lot out of it; I could trust my intuition to help me remember selected parts of the dreams, which, no matter how small, I could gain from. Whether or not the full dream from which these fragments came would have conveyed the same message I'll never know. It could be that the message would have been lost amid all the other messages inherent in detailed dreams, and that my intuitive self, realizing that, and especially wanting me to get *this* message, set it up in just this way.

Since that first experience I pay careful attention to dream fragments, whether they are a single word or a sentence or two. And invariably they have meaning, not only as a unit, but in conjunction with other fragments or even entire dreams. For instance, one morning I came up with three fragments: (1) ISBN, (2) an elegant if rundown beach cottage, and (3) "whirling around and hitting at air." After that was a short but complete dream involving a boat. And finally another fragment: "Shoofly pie and apple pan-dowdy," the words to a popular song of many years ago.

ISBN is a book identification prefix, and I decided it was also a label for the author me. The beach cottage was what the label referred to—my self-image as an elegant if rundown beach house. This fit the way I was feeling about myself at the time. The "whirling around and hitting at air" image to me evoked Don Quixote (battling the windmill), which further led to an image of an imprisoned princess—a part of me I have glimpsed but been a bit reluctant to accept. The dream about the boat then dealt with these two self-images in a meaningful way. Had it not been for the pinpointing of these fragments, I might not have recognized these aspects of myself in the boat dream, for though they were there, they did not stand out clearly in the way the fragments did. Following the boat dream, the "shoofly pie" fragment evoked some memories I won't go into but which lent a fitting, upbeat end to the sequence.

One advantage to fragments is that they are short, and thus it takes less time to work through to a message with them than it does with complete dreams. It could well be that if you are remembering only fragments it is because you believe it is too time-consuming to work with long dreams and yet you'd feel guilty if you did remember a long dream but didn't work with it.

In any case, write down those dream fragments. They can be very enlightening. And look through old dream material for fragments you may not have paid much attention to, and see what you can do with them now. Try the mind-mapping technique if you get stuck. This can of course be used with entire dreams, putting various images in circles and seeing how they relate to one another. However, a dream fully remembered will usually present images juxtaposed in an already meaningful way, and so it usually isn't necessary to mind-map them.

When fragments occur during the same dreaming session as a fully remembered dream see if you can establish a meaning connection among all of them. Good luck.

Exercise #46

Whether we experience terror or rapture, our most memorable dreams are invariably the most emotional. Jon remembered his "blob" dream years later because of its emotional impact, in this case, negative. It fits in the "nightmare" category. Dreams of rapture, which often involve meeting and merging with the higher self, have no generic title, but are equally memorable. Nightmares invariably present us with a challenge, "night raptures" with a sense of power and divinity. Meeting the challenge of a nightmare often brings us to this same exalted state. We saw how Jon, challenged by his "blob" dream, performed a ritual that transformed the negative energy into positive. By immolating the blob in a drawing, he was able to let go of the beliefs connected with it and to believe instead in his creative power. From this perspective the two types of dreams, though they seem to us in space-time to be opposites, are both about the same thing: power. Both, in their evocation of strong emotions, give us a memorable experience of the power within.

But what about our less memorable dreams? Especially, what about our less memorable negative dreams? Seth has said that nightmares come after a long period of frustration. They're a means of getting our attention, of shocking us into dealing with issues in our lives causing ever-increasing stress. If we're able to learn from our everyday dreams, we don't need something drastic like nightmares to finally alert us to what is going on inside.

We've all had frustrating dreams. Simply understanding the dreams' message—that we're frustrated—is in itself helpful and results in change. But an additional way to deal with frustrating dreams is to rewrite them. This is especially true of recurring dreams. Say you dream night after night of being on a treadmill going around and around, getting nowhere. Or take a less obvious example of a series of dreams with different events and settings but always ending in the same inconclusive way—you don't accomplish a task you set out to accomplish, you can't find the house you are looking for, you cannot run fast enough to catch up with whatever it is you are trying to catch, you keep finding yourself faced with the same puzzle you thought you solved already, you replay the same argument with different people. In waking life you may not be aware of any particular frustrations, but in nightly dramas they're showing up regularly, gently but firmly reminding you that here is an area of disharmony within. If you ignore such dreams, they're likely to become more intense until they reach the nightmare stage. If you acknowledge and understand them, you automatically get the energy moving in a more positive direction. And if you actively use your imagination to envision a different outcome, you speed up those results.

Physical reality emerges out of a network of interacting areas of significance, meaning-filled energy vibrating in sync, creating and recreating its own frequency, its own unique world. In order for a given probable event to materialize, it must set up reverberations of meaning with other probable events, creating a psychological atmosphere within which it will "make sense" in physical form. The more nuances of meaning contained in an event, the higher the likelihood of its occurrence. As Seth says repeatedly, we get what we concentrate on. Concentration is not necessarily a matter of intense conscious focus, but more often of looking at an area of meaning in a number of ways, adding nuances to it. Winning the lottery is an example. We may focus intensely on this goal, and when we don't reach it (along with millions of others), we decide we don't get what we concentrate on after all. But what we don't realize is that every time we think about winning the lottery we remind ourselves that we are "poor" right now, that we can never be rich, that we don't deserve to be, that something is wrong with having money, or simply that it is impossible to "beat" such odds. Instead of focusing on the significance of winning we are focusing on and adding a number of nuances to the significance of losing.

So, when doing this exercise, do it as a playful exploration of meaning rather than as a serious attempt to focus on a particular outcome. In imagining an outcome you explore meaning in one way. By writing down what you imagine you explore it in a different way. You might also dance the outcome, paint the outcome, and sculpt it. Each time you'll get a different view of it, adding to its meaning and its attractive power. You may even discover you already had it in your power to bring about that outcome and that you have done so in other areas of your life. In this way you strengthen your "winning" network. Through imaginatively changing frustrating dreams into satisfying ones you add meaning to satisfaction.

Exercise #47

Seth often made spontaneous visits to Jane Roberts's ESP classes, as chronicled by Sue Watkins in her two volumes of *Conversations with Seth*. One moment Jane or the students would be talking, and the next, Jane/Seth would remove her glasses, slapping them down on the coffee table. Then the Seth personality would take over, bantering with the students, offering advice, suggesting exercises for them to do.

During an ESP class in May 1974, the class had been talking with Seth about his statement that "there are no divisions to the self." One student wanted to know why, if there were no divisions to the self, one could love someone and hate someone at the same time. Another student agreed. "You mean we're doomed to feel twenty thousand ways about everything because that's the way the 'undivided' self *is?*"

It was then that Seth told the class to ask for a "True Dream from the Gates of Horn," a title that came from the ancient Egyptians. He said such a dream would help harmonize those conflicting "divisions" of the self the students had been talking about.

Sue said she felt surprisingly skeptical about the suggestion. As she was driving home from the class, she found herself inwardly arguing, What's the use of a suggestion anyway, since if you don't really like the suggestion, then you won't use it? Your self will protect you from it. On the other hand, was she feeling resistant simply because she didn't want to harmonize the conflicting sides of herself, preferring indecision to resolution?

As it turned out, she needn't have worried, for "True Dreams from the Gates of Horn" became for her and other members of the class not only some of the most meaningful, but also some of the most enjoyable dreams they'd recorded. Everyone agreed that the "TD/GH" dreams were completely different from any others they'd had.

One woman said her TD/GH dreams all dealt with nature, merging it with the dream reality in a way difficult to describe, but leaving her with the felt sense of "the source she springs from."

Sue herself had a set of dreams filled with strange juxtaposed scenes ending with one in which her aunt shows her a bedroom in her grandmother's house, which had been Sue's as a child. She says: ". . . and then I feel this room being created in my past—I *feel* it spilling out of this dream . . . and backwards into physical 'fact' where it becomes a familiar memory. . . . But I *know* that [it is being] created NOW, in this TD/GH."*

* Susan M. Watkins, *Conversations with Seth: Volume II* (New York: Prentice-Hall, 1981), p. 416.

Symbols have power. In this case the symbol is a phrase resonating back to ancient Egypt: True Dreams from the Gates of Horn. And its harmonizing power was felt by all of the dreamers.

Sue says that class members came to use "True Dreams" as a call for help, when they felt out of touch with their inner being, when they wanted to restore a sense of harmony. Such requests always resulted in vivid, soul-stirring answers. One student remarked, "You don't ask unless you *really want to know.*"

Ask for a True Dream from the Gates of Horn, then, only when you "really want to know," and be prepared for a powerful experience.

Exercise #48

What some writers call "lucid dreaming" Seth simply calls "coming awake" in the dream state. We can train ourselves to awaken within the dream state by coming to understand that the entity who dreams is the same entity who participates in space-time. We have all had experiences in waking reality (Seth says we could have a lot more) of directing or "altering" our consciousness in different ways—of concentrating sharply or of letting our mind wander; of feeling hypnotized by music or impassioned by a speech. Whatever state we're in, it's familiar to us, we recognize it as ours, the consciousness a property of our being. But when consciousness "crosses the line" into the dream state, we tend to see the differences in organization and perception as an indication that a different consciousness has "taken over," rather than an indication that the changes have reached a certain degree of difference from the waking state. Just realizing we are still in charge, still the possessors of the consciousness involved, will make it possible for the "us" we identify with to become much more aware and creative while in the dream state.

As a preliminary exercise to coming awake within dreams, see how closely you can emulate dream consciousness when awake. Dream consciousness is very familiar to us, accessible to the waking us to a greater degree than we may realize. It's just that in material reality we use time and space as a means of getting around and experiencing events, while in dream reality we use *intent*. In dreams, time and space still exist, but they don't operate in the same way. Rather than traveling for a certain period of time through a certain amount of space in order to get to where we want, in the dream state the mere act of intending to get there brings the place to us. It may feel as if we have gone to it, but that is because of our space-time orientation. It is more accurate to the dream state to say that the place sprang up before us due to our intent for it to do so. And the same is true of events. In the dream state we neither go to them or through them, but attract them to us through our intent.

Imagine yourself in an environment where time and space don't operate, where through your intent you can bring to you whatever you want—people, objects, places, events. Practice doing this and notice especially how you feel as it's happening. The more you can feel it in your imagination, the better you will be prepared for the experience in your dreams. By bringing your consciousness several degrees closer to the dream state than you have ever done before, you will be better prepared to take an active role within your dreams, knowing what to expect and how it feels to operate by intent.

Exercise #49

What is common sense? I ask this because I suspect a lot of people, if asked whether dreams are real, would give the "common sense" answer that they are not. "Obviously dreams aren't real. Use your common sense." Or, "Your question is ridiculous. Everyone knows dreams aren't real."

But not everyone does know. To children not yet indoctrinated with our prevailing belief system it is obvious that dreams are real. Their own experience tells them so. To accept the notion that they're not would seem to go against all common sense. We all know what the experience of dreaming feels like, whether or not we remember our dreams, and we all know that while we are immersed in a dream it is utterly real to us. When we do remember our dreams they very often strike us as bizarre, but at the time they didn't seem so. I often used to think while dreaming that I was in a space-time situation, often with people I knew, only to realize after I'd awakened that the circumstances of the dream were impossible in waking life, that the familiar people really weren't people I know "here"—which didn't keep me from having the same feeling the next time I dreamed.

Once I learned to come awake within dreams, my perspective shifted. I found myself within the dream recognizing that what was happening was impossible in space-time terms, aware that much of what I was experiencing was bizarre. Not that the dream felt any less real to me; in fact, quite the opposite. While before, the dream seemed real because of its similarity to space-time (and only on awakening did I realize its dissimilarities), now, it had a reality of its own apart from space-time, and within the dream I came to notice its special features and to play with them. I came to see clearly that this was indeed a different focus of consciousness, a different reality, and not the distorted mentalized version of space-time our "common sense" tells us it is.

It seems to me that understanding dreams to be real is crucial if we are truly to expand in consciousness (which Seth tells us the species is ready for). Though there are limits to how far our consciousness can stretch while we have part of our being in space-time, still we limit ourselves unnecessarily through our belief that physical experience is more real and more valid than psychological experience. As long as we believe that consciousness has one true focus, that it is situated in one body, that it begins at birth and ends at death, we will continue to "discover" this, even as we try to explore our dreams. If, however, we can learn to come awake within our dreams, experiencing with more awareness the consciousness that is ours unconstrained by time or space, our belief in a narrowly constricted self will fall away and we will come to see ourselves as multidimensional beings using consciousness in all different ways.

Before going to sleep give yourself instructions to come awake while dreaming, and to realize you are in the dreaming mode. Tell yourself you will feel comfortable and familiar with this mode, having experienced in your imagination how it feels to operate by intent. Tell yourself you will feel free within this reality to create whatever you want, using intent to attract to you the experiences you choose. Write your experiences down when you awaken.

Exercise #50

I've never seen an exercise quite like this one, suggested by Seth in *Unknown Reality*. He says we are used to examining our dream state while awake but not to examining our waking state while dreaming. True enough. The reason being, I think, because we identify with the ego in space-time. It is "us," and everything else is "not us." Asking us to examine our waking state from the dream state is like asking us to become what we are not (a dream entity) and then to look at ourselves (the ego) objectively, from the outside.

Coming awake in the dream state helps dispel this narrow sense of identification, for we realize we are still us and yet not the us of normal waking life. We realize that a shift in consciousness creates a different being with a different worldview—and that being is still us. We identify ourselves more as consciousness and less as a form that consciousness takes.

This exercise, particularly, helps us to see that we are more than we think we are by giving us a new perspective on our "official" space-time reality. It involves identifying closely with the sleeping self in the dream state, with the focus of consciousness whose normal reality is the dream world.

You can practice this switch of identification in waking life by choosing a person you care about and want to understand better, then imagining yourself being that person, viewing the world from his or her perspective. See how it feels to make this switch and remember this feeling in your dream.

Tell yourself before going to sleep that as usual you will come awake in the dream state. Then suggest to yourself that this time you will identify with the dreaming self, that you are familiar with this feeling of identification, and you will view waking reality from this perspective. Waking reality will become a dream world to this self you identify with, and as such "unreal."

Seth often says that if we can see the objects and events of waking life not as facts, immutable and fixed in concrete, but rather as symbols, representing a playfully creative consciousness eager to experience material existence, we can then take a more playful and consciously creative role in our space-time lives.

Exercise #51

A remembered dream is like a snapshot, or a series of snapshots, each image taken from the context of an endless flow of activity and, when "viewed," given a context befitting our waking beliefs and feelings. Since our purpose in "taking" the photo is to use it in waking life, we give it a space-time context, remembering little of the original dream environment. In this sense, our dream reality—what we remember of it—reflects back to us our present feelings and beliefs.

But it's a two-way street. Sometimes, in the dream state, we take surprising snapshots which, when viewed in space-time, don't fit into our accustomed context, requiring us to change some beliefs in order to accommodate this new view of reality. In that sense, our space-time reality reflects our dream reality.

The more conscious we become within the dream reality, the more we'll notice, by bringing back snapshots bound to give us an expanded view of waking reality, and how we automatically change it. Because in space-time we believe ourselves to be limited in various ways, we tend to see limitations in our dreams. In this exercise you are going to expand inner space.

Before going to sleep, tell yourself you will come awake while dreaming, that you will be aware that you are dreaming, and that you will feel comfortable navigating in that system of reality. Tell yourself you will remember your explorations when you awaken.

In the dream try to expand whatever space you find yourself in. If you are in a room, make it larger, go into another room, and another, and another— make them all larger. Look at the scene outside the window, step into it, expand it. If you are going down a street, follow it as far as you can, with it reaching out before you; then turn a corner and encounter a new environment and stretch it out, expand it, feel its ever-increasing spaciousness, feel it expanding into infinity, so that nowhere does that environment end.

When you write down your dream in the morning, try especially to recapture the feeling of spaciousness you had, of your ability to stretch space at will, to expand. The feeling alone, whatever the images, will have an impact on your waking reality. Retain that feeling and see how your experience of space changes to reflect the experience of your dream. Does your bedroom feel bigger? Is the horizon farther away? Do you have more room?

Exercise #52

The Senoi were a peaceful society living in the remote jungles of Malaysia when discovered by sociologists in the early 1900s. They fascinated researchers because of their cooperative, nonviolent lifestyle. A tolerant and creative people, they had flexible attitudes toward marriage and sexuality, and were free of neuroses and anxiety. Their psychological maturity was so remarkable that one ethnographer described them as the most civilized people he'd ever seen—despite their primitive living conditions.

The Senoi attached great importance to dreams, using them as a natural source of therapy and information. Jungian analysts and others have incorporated Senoi ideas and techniques in their counseling and group work. The Senoi understood the precognitive aspect of dreams and realized that many incipient conflicts in waking life could be worked out in dreams, "before they happened."

From an early age children were encouraged to participate actively within their dreams, coming awake within them and taking control of whatever situation they were in, transforming any frightening or negative actions and images into positive ones. If a child had a nightmare, he or she was told to have the same dream the next night and this time to confront the frightening aspects of the dream and make friends with them. Friends in a dream were considered of great value, to be called upon by the dreamer for guidance and support.

When a dream seemed to be precognitive, say, one in which the dreamer quarreled with a playmate, the parents instructed the child to discuss this with their waking-life friend, to nip a possible conflict in the bud before it appeared in space-time.

Senoi children were taught to carry all dreams to a successful and enjoyable conclusion. Thus, if a child dreamed of falling from a cliff and awakened before landing, the father or mother would congratulate the youngster on his or her fine flying dream and urge a pleasurable continuation and completion of the dream next time. Since no imagery in dreams was considered shameful, incestuous, or taboo, children were encouraged to amplify "libidinous" dreams. Adults thoroughly approved of these "love dreams," instructing children to take delight in erotic play and to culminate in orgasm. How different Freud's theories would have been had he worked with these people!

The next few exercises will be based on Senoi techniques. In this one, come awake within your dream and become aware of any fears you have and the symbols associated with them. Focus on these one by one and in each case transform the symbol into a positive one. Make it your friend.

Exercise #53

A friend I'll call Connie had a long series of ever more detailed dreams it was my pleasure to read. What I found particularly interesting about the dreams was the evolution within them of a wise, kind, helpful guide. In the first dream where this figure occurred, it was in the guise of a wise old man. In a later one it appeared as an old woman passing through. In the next one the old woman suddenly transformed within the dream into a lovely twin self. It was in the next dream that the image, shimmeringly beautiful, gave herself a name. ("Aroara" was the way Connie spelled it; she was unaware of the dawn goddess whose name is of similar spelling.)

From then on this wise and friendly guide appeared in all of Connie's dreams in the same guise. She always showed up in the last act of the drama, and her role was to explain what had gone before and to reassure and comfort the dreaming Connie. As time went on Connie could imaginatively evoke this guide of hers while awake.

This persona might variously be called "higher self," "spirit guide," "soul," "source," "self," or something else. Some might liken it to a channeled entity, met first in dreams then accessible in waking life. However you choose to view this creative, wise personification of wisdom and love, he or she is a wonderful friend to have, as the Senoi well knew. There is no evidence to suggest that they viewed the friends in dreams in any of the above ways, but they recognized the value of cultivating friendly dream figures to give them assistance and moral support within dreams. They also realized that dreams spilled over into waking life and as such were a playground not only for the resolution of probable conflicts but also for the creation of positive forces in waking life.

In your dreams, take note of wise and friendly figures—those who help you out, give you advice, comfort, and reassure. It may not always seem appropriate to you, within the dream, to stop and relate with a friendly entity, but know that anytime you want to call upon this being again, all you need do is intend to, and he or she will appear before you. You may find this friend in many guises and prefer it this way. Or, as was the case with Connie, you may find the dream helper evolving into a super-powered image. Whether you cultivate a number of dream friends or have a favorite, the positive effect from this source will manifest itself in waking life.

Exercise #54

In the literature about dreaming, accounts of out-of-body experiences abound. Jane Roberts herself had many such experiences and wrote about them in *Dreams and the Projection of Consciousness.** The original title for that book was *Dreams and Out-of-Body Experiences,* but it was changed because it was thought that some people were put off by the idea of "going out of body," either because it was too far-fetched or downright scary. "Projection of consciousness" had a more authoritative and thus comforting ring to it.

Technically speaking, all dreams are projections of consciousness, all dreams are out-of-body experiences. When we dream, our consciousness shifts gears, creating a different system of reality containing elements of both physical and nonphysical. Though the body's sensual apparatus still registers—sight and sound especially—the body lies dormant as consciousness travels. It is in this sense that all dreams involve a projection of consciousness, an experience out of the body.

But both terms have come to be used in a specialized way to mean those dreams in which we are consciously aware of leaving the body (we may see it lying on the bed as we hover nearby), in which we take off flying, in which to varying degrees we control our flight. Some people have reported tentative flying experiments in their dreams where they cautiously "rolled out" of their bodies and ascended a few feet above it, but then looked back down and were a bit fearful about getting permanently separated, which was enough to "pull" them back. Some people report waking within the dreams to find themselves flying, getting scared, and instantly finding themselves back in the body. Some report being able to maintain their flight for some time and to control it—up and down, through walls, etc.—to some extent. And then there are those who have had flying dreams all of their lives and can bring them on at will and explore where they choose. Finally there are those who have never had a dream in which they perceived themselves flying out of body.

The Senoi valued flying dreams for their fun and adventure, and no doubt because they realized that sense of fun and adventure would be translated into waking life. They helped their children to recognize potential flying dreams (such as dreams of falling) and encouraged them to take flight in their dreams.

I can well remember my first flying dream, when I first became aware in the dream that I had the choice to fly. I was at the end of a thin, swaying branch atop a very tall, leafless tree, looking over at others in the same situation on other trees. The wind came up and the branch I was on began whipping about as I gradually lost my grip. I looked way, way down below to where I would

* Jane Roberts, *Dreams and the Projection of Consciousness* (Dallas: Still Point Press, 1986).

soon be going as I slid along the branch and finally off the end. I began falling toward the ground. But right away I noticed how slowly I was going. I wasn't plummeting toward imminent death at all: I was floating! Once I realized this, I looked up, spread my arms and ascended into the sky.

I awakened the next morning exhilarated and with hazy memories of other dreams in which I had been in similar situations but clung desperately to my tree. It felt like a real breakthrough that I had finally accepted the idea of flying—which was all it took to bring flying into the dream. I also had the distinct feeling that I had been gently coached into it. The part of me who wanted to fly had finally succeeded in getting the more conservative part of me to let go and let it happen.

If you have never experienced a flying dream, and would like to, next time you come awake within your dream, decide you are going to fly. If all portions of your psyche are willing, you will! It's simply a matter of intent and desire unmarred by beliefs/fears to the contrary.

If you have experienced flying in dreams and enjoyed it, but do not seem to be able to summon the experience at will, next time you come awake within the dream decide that this time you will do it.

In either case, take note of the sense of exhilaration and freedom flying dreams invariably bring, and consciously cultivate that feeling in waking life. Allow that exhilaration and freedom to spill out into space-time.

Exercise #55

The Senoi would seem to be living proof that we create our waking reality largely in the dream world. By the time they were adults the members of this Malaysian culture had all learned to create pleasurable dreams for themselves, dreams in which any conflicts were dealt with and resolved, where all events led to a satisfying completion. And, according to many researchers, their waking life mirrored their dreams: They were a peaceful, cooperative, emotionally mature, sexually uninhibited, happy people.

Let this final exercise based on the Senoi teachings, then, leave you with the idea that it is not only possible but highly desirable to bring all dreams to a pleasurable conclusion. Let your conflicts be resolved, let your enemies become your friends, let your friends become your guides, let your spirit soar. And finally, remember that even in flying dreams, your body is participating. Don't forget your body. If in waking life you are having sexual conflicts, bring them into the dream state, and in the playful spirit of dreams, resolve them. Carry that sense of completion with you back into the waking state. Become aware of how the pleasurable feelings generated in dreams remain with you in the waking state, how they change your outlook, your worldview, your very reality. Dreams work!

Exercise #56

Every "level" of reality is a mirror of All That Is. Just as All That Is dreamed reality into existence to "begin" with, so too do we continually dream ourselves into existence in space-time, mirroring this Primal Activity. Just as All That Is continues to evolve along with its creations, so too do we. Physical reality as we know and experience it has evolved out of the dreams of all of the entities choosing to have some portion of their existence "here." From the first time the idea of physical reality appeared as a dream, all of its possibilities were born as well. But exploring these possibilities was a gradual building process, forwarded by dreams.

In *Dreams, Evolution, and Value Fulfillment** Seth talks of the "Sleepwalkers," our human predecessors, whose consciousness was focused primarily in the dream world, where they practiced and learned how to operate within the still unfamiliar constraints of space and time. To them, "waking" reality was dreamlike, bizarre. Just as we can train ourselves to become more conscious within dream reality, so they gradually trained themselves to manipulate within this reality. Such taken-for-granted activities as breathing and walking they learned through trial and error, first in the dream world, then here.

The better these Sleepwalkers became at manipulating within space-time, the more attention they gave to it, and the more time per day they spent focused within it. Eventually, a part of their consciousness (later to be called the ego) came to identify itself with space-time, to perceive itself as taking up space, having boundaries all about it that gave it a shape (later to be called a body), and having a duration in time (from birth to death). In order for this part of the Sleepwalker's consciousness to keep this focus, for it to remember who it decided it was in space-time, it had to put limits on its simultaneous awareness of itself as essentially spaceless and timeless. (This became the brain's job.) Thus its original world beyond dreams became less and less accessible, more and more unreal. A new species of consciousness arose who walked when awake and dreamed when asleep, and the Sleepwalkers were no more. They had served their purpose in forwarding the evolution of physical consciousness.

But though the new species lost awareness of its creative learning ground, this ground continues to operate as fully as ever. Most of the learning taking place on earth originates in dreams. Human babies sleep a lot precisely because they have so much to learn, or relearn, as they adapt to earth existence. They

* Jane Roberts, *Dreams, Evolution, and Value Fulfillment* (New York: Prentice Hall Press, 1986) pps. 166 and 186.

dream of crawling before they crawl, of speaking before they speak, even of crying before they cry.

And so do we: We dream of speaking a foreign language before we speak it, of making that golf swing before we make it, of writing that letter before it gets written. No longer need we be conscious of our breathing in order to keep breathing, as the early Sleepwalkers had to, because they discovered that this and the multitude of other so-called mechanical activities of the body could be dealt with by another species of consciousness that evolved: body consciousness. Body consciousness evolved along with ego consciousness but took a different line of development. It has maintained an intimate conscious connection with its roots, relegating to the ego the job of "staying awake" in space-time and interpreting that reality. Body consciousness takes its cues from ego consciousness in reality creating, each instant exuberantly producing a body perfectly in tune with the worldview of the ego, a reflection of its beliefs.

The dreams that we dream—at least the majority of those that we remember and all of those out of which our reality is created—also take their cue from ego consciousness. The ego has unlimited say in creating the space-time reality from which other portions of the psyche can partake only indirectly. Of course, it consults, collaborates, and cocreates with other egos as well as other physically oriented consciousnesses: Together these consciousnesses create a mass reality within the context of which the individual entities have their own personal realities. And to an extent that varies greatly among individuals, the ego also listens and strives to fulfill the values of its inner being. But ultimately it is the decision of the ego that determines the space-time reality of a given psyche. It is the attitudes and beliefs of the ego that determine the choice of probable events run through in dreams and that determine the choice from among those probable events of the ones to become actualized.

The ego has an awesome task and it needs all the help it can get. The more we can take advantage of that wise voice within, the more active and conscious a role we take within our dreams; to that extent we will realize not only how much responsibility we really do have but also how much wisdom and creativity there is for us to draw from. It is time for us to "come home."

Think of a skill you would like to develop—speaking French, playing golf, building boats, managing a business, selling ideas. Choose something you believe you could be good at and that fits into an envisioned future—something, perhaps, you have wanted to learn from an expert. Ask your expert within to instruct you in this skill. Before going to sleep each night ask for one dream in which you are taught and can practice this skill. Tell yourself you will come awake within this dream and take a conscious role in your learning.

If you are already taking French lessons, or managing a business or whatever else it is you want to become skilled at, you should notice an immediate improvement in that skill, a greater facility, whether or not you remember dreaming about it. If you have yet to learn about or practice the skill, you will probably discover "reminders" of the skill in waking life. If you want to write a novel, you may find yourself thinking about and having the urge to write down anecdotes or character sketches; you may find yourself attracted to certain types of novels or a particular writer you feel a common bond with. You may start keeping a journal or write more letters to friends. You may begin meeting other people who want to write. Taking space-time action will be up to you. But the groundwork is being laid in your dreams.

Exercise #57

Even from the perspective of the ego, most of our space-time experience is nonmaterial. Our minds work constantly to "make sense" of whatever happens to us physically, running through a huge repository of probable events in order to fit the official event into an understandable context. Of all the things that could happen to us, only a small percentage actually do, but we still experience many other possibilities in our mind. What does not happen to us is as significant an experience to us as what does, as integral an experience to space-time as physical events.

This concept is important to remember in working with dreams, for it is on the dream level that we experience the overall context of events, and on the dream level that certain events are chosen for manifestation. According to Seth, we could make a lot more conscious use of dreams for therapeutic purposes, playing out in dreams our conflicts so that there is no need for them to be manifested in physical reality. The Senoi knew this, which is why they trained themselves to bring their dreams to pleasurable conclusions, defusing conflict before it sprang up in space-time.

One form psychological conflict takes in space-time is illness, and it was specifically illness Seth was referring to when talking about the therapeutic use of dreams. Illness is the body's symbolic way of expressing disharmony, a disharmony that could be dealt with in dreams through suggestion.

He uses the example of aggressive tendencies. Usually we're not allowed to express these in space-time and so we repress them and become ill. However, when we're aware that we're feeling angry or hostile about something, we can suggest that we experience aggressiveness within a dream as well as suggest that we learn to understand our aggressions by watching ourselves in the dream as if it were a play we'd written with ourselves as both actor and audience. If we come to understand what we're doing within the dream, this "action" is just as significant as a space-time event, and the waking ego will understand too (for the dreaming and waking consciousness are the same consciousness) and won't need to create more "lessons" for itself in this area.

Seth makes the cautionary comment that we not suggest dreams in which our aggression is directed against a person in space-time (i.e., the one we're angry at). It is not the person who is the problem but our aggressive feelings we need to deal with. We should never suggest a dream for ourselves in which we harm another space-time person. Rather, the idea is to suggest a therapeutic dream dealing with particular tendencies in us we want help with. Our aggressive feelings are the villain, not the character in space-time who agreed to be in our play so that we could learn about ourselves from it.

Another way we can consciously use dreams to heal our bodies is to ask a dream simply to let us know what needs to be done to take care of an illness or pain, ask it to uncover conflicts we are unaware of, or ask it to give us understanding of the conflict so that healing can take place. We can make much more use of our dreams in this way than most of us presently do.

And of course, since dream consciousness and waking consciousness are one, if we are feeling frustrated in waking life, we often have frustrating dreams. Once we see the connection we can either ask our dream to resolve the frustration or ask for a joyful dream, which in itself will give us a different perspective on life and reduce our frustration.

Exercise #58

The consciousness of each one of us, according to Seth, is a "literally endless" energy gestalt composed of innumerable points of consciousness that together make up our identity, that form our significance. In space-time terms, this gestalt could be "dispersed throughout the universe, with galaxies between" and that identity, that significance, still be maintained. At the same time, those points of consciousness are involved in other gestalts, forming other identities, other significances equally as indestructible, whatever the distance between them.

This means that every portion of our being, each point of consciousness comprising our significance and identity, also comprises portions of other beings, of other gestalts, of other significant identities. In space-time terms we could compare points of consciousness to molecules of matter. Each molecule has its own identity and significance, and also participates in a "larger" identity that is continually changing form in space and time. (That it is perceived as only one "thing" at "once" is what makes it part of our system.) A molecule of air, when in our lungs, is part of us, part of our identity and significance. Once we breathe it out it becomes "air" again, or it is absorbed by the grass to become "grass," or goes up into the sky to become "cloud." We breathe in—and aerate blood and body with what "used to be" portions of other beings. I once read that every human on earth during a lifetime breathes in at least one molecule from the breath of every other. Even in space-time terms it can be seen that we are all a part of one another.

In waking life we are so used to thinking in terms of spatial and temporal boundaries that this mixing and merging of identities goes unperceived. But in dreams, once again because they to varying extents transcend space and time, this merging becomes more visible. Not only do we dream of ourselves and others in different human guises (which may or may not have space-time counterparts), but we dream of half-animal humans, half-human animals, of nature sprites, of "living" objects, of all kinds of "impossible" entities. As Seth says, in dreams we get much closer to the true nature of reality than we ordinarily do in space-time.

It is because of this basic oneness of All That Is, because of the fact that every bit of consciousness "shares significance" with every other, that we can keep space-time running. When Seth says we share information in dreams, he's not talking about a meeting where each individual entity participating in space-time reports to the others and then they all come to a policy decision. Rather, within dreams we *become* one another. We let loose our focus on one identity and become aware of ourselves as participating in other gestalts, in other identities. In this sense we don't need to share information since there is nothing outside of ourselves, outside of consciousness, to share with. We directly experience, directly know what every other entity knows—all of us become one entity, one consciousness, the mass consciousness comprising physical reality. It is this experience that comprises our information, all the information we'll ever need to keep space-time running.

So-called primitive man, whose ego consciousness was not as developed as ours, often experienced this melding of consciousness, becoming a portion of the tree or the stream or the animal through a shift in focus, knowing intuitively that his identification as a human remained inviolate. As our species developed its specialization—an exploration of self and not-self as detached, separate beings—it lost this flexibility of consciousness and, ironically enough, came to fear the loss of that very identity it came best to know.

Seth says we are now ready to reverse this separating trend. Having learned what we have from this perspective, as a species we are now ready to allow our waking consciousness more flexibility, to recognize and to affirm our identification with all of being, to bring into space-time that all-knowing consciousness we meet each night in dreams. The better acquainted we become in our dreams with this form that our consciousness takes, the better able we will be to bring it into space-time.

Suggest to yourself that you will come awake within your dreams and that you will experience a melding of identity with other earthly species. Tell yourself you will be unafraid to "leave behind" your ego and become "something else." Reassure yourself that you do this all the time, even in waking life you do this, "unconsciously" identifying with a friend, your children, a pet; with trees, clouds, sky, and wind; with characters in books, much loved belongings—car, violin, sculpture; with emotions carrying you out of "yourself." You do this and still remain yourself, forever and inviolably yourself. Suggest to yourself that in your dream you will consciously decide to project your consciousness in this way, to meld and become a part of another being, partaking of the knowledge and feelings of that being. Tell yourself that you will remember this dream in the morning and that you will carry with you the strong feeling of conscious identification as a part of all nature you experienced in the dream. Bring it into space-time.

Exercise #59

My same friend Connie related a dream to me that began with one character, a woman, who had a life-threatening illness, perhaps cancer. Very soon the dream split into two segments that Connie found herself alternately tuning into. In one segment she observed and experienced the character succumbing to her illness, believing she had no other choice but death. In the other segment she experienced the "same" character choosing not to die but to overcome her illness. Toward the end the two segments merged once again, as did the two characters, the one who chose life "winning out" over the one who gave up.

This dream is interesting on many levels. It was especially interesting to Connie because she has twin daughters who are "mirror-image" twins; that is, one is left-handed and the other right-handed, one's hair naturally parts on the right, the other's on the left, and so on. Not only that, while one is verbal, outgoing, and optimistic, the other is quiet, withdrawn, and pessimistic. She saw this dream as addressing some challenges she was then facing in waking life in connection with her daughters and their influence on one another as it pertained to her.

The dream is also interesting in the way it shows how beliefs create our realities. Clearly the message on this level is that we do have a choice in what we believe and thus in the reality we create for ourselves. Also, depending on who is interpreting the dream, it could contain the message that, whatever "life-death" or "good-evil" conflict might be going on, it will have a "happy" ending. Or, simply that answers and solutions lie within us. No doubt other interpretations occurred to you.

The dream is interesting also in that it illustrates how probability systems interact. Any time "here on earth" we are confronted with an important decision that will drastically affect our life, and any time we then make that decision, at that point a probable being is "born" who in his or her system of reality explores what would have happened had a different decision been made. The ending of the dream also shows how probable selves can influence one another even to the point where they once again merge farther down the road. We'll be taking a detailed look at probable selves in the next chapter.

Still another interesting aspect of the dream is its multidimensional character, with two distinct but intertwined realities going on at the same time. Connie told me that while she was dreaming she felt herself participating simultaneously in both, but when it came to writing the dream down, she found herself focusing on first one segment of the dream and then the other. As Seth says, in waking reality we are not neurologically equipped to handle two realities, two identities, two focuses of consciousness at once, and so either we remember one dream as two or three or four, or one dream predominates and the others are fragmentary. Or, as in comparatively rare cases like this one, we recognize it all happened at once, but cannot describe it that way.

A few talented dreamers, Jane Roberts among them, have reported double, even triple dreams in which the dreamer was aware of two or more simultaneous realities and/or perspectives on reality during the dream. As we saw in the last exercise, we do have many identities and participate in many realities all at once. In the last exercise I asked you to focus on one of these "other" identities within the dream, experiencing reality as that entity. In this, the culminating exercise of this chapter, I'd like you to create a double or triple dream for yourself in order to get the experience of a consciousness simultaneously embracing more than one identity.

Once again, give yourself the suggestion that you will awaken within your dream, aware that you are dreaming. Tell yourself that this time you will be aware of two or more areas of action going on at the same time, that you are open to whatever form comes to you, that you will take in what is happening and understand it and remember it the next day. Tell yourself that within your dream, outside of space-time constraints, you will be able to experience simultaneous realities without difficulty and that their related meaning will be clear to you. Tell yourself you will let your consciousness expand so as to include simultaneous realities. Tell yourself that consciousness is by nature multidimensional and you are going to experience that multidimensionality tonight, in your dreams.

7

Expanding Waking Consciousness

You can . . . allow your 'dream self' greater expression in the waking state. This can be done through techniques that are largely connected with creativity. Creativity connects waking and dreaming reality, and is in itself a threshold in which the waking and dreaming selves merge to form constructs that belong equally to each reality.

The Nature of the Psyche, pp. 140–1.

It's really very simple (if not always easy): Since it is in dreams that we experience and select events for physical actualization, then if we wish to become more conscious reality creators, an obvious way to do so is to first become more aware in the dream state (the purpose of the last chapter), and second, to cultivate in waking life, to a much greater extent than is now the case, the perspective consciousness takes within dreams (the purpose of this chapter). If we can develop the ability to view waking life as the richly symbolic world that it is, and see beyond the symbols to their underlying meaning, then we can not only understand our space-time selves better but take an active conscious role in our reality, using symbols as tools, playfully, to build our lives.

"Playfully" is a key word. Seth has said many times that we cannot hope to experience when awake the more flexible and expansive consciousness characteristic of the dream state if we take a sternly disciplined, problem-solving approach—the Scientific Method. This approach may have its uses in space-time (though to a much greater extent than they realize, says Seth, scientists bring into the process their beliefs, whims, and intuitions), but certainly not in an exploration of the psyche/mind/whole self. If we don't delight in surprises, welcome the unexpected, and take joy in the absurd, then we're not *experiencing* expanded consciousness at all. And, as Seth says, experience is knowledge. We know, not through the words created in order to deal with space-time, but through what is behind the words, the feeling of significance, the exhilaration of insight, the intuitive sense of rightness, the experience of being.

The waking state of consciousness most akin to the dreaming state is active imagination, in which while fully alert we let our images flow, experiencing and observing events simultaneously, making instant associations based

121

on felt significance rather than "logic." It is in this state that creativity has its greatest range, where fruitful ideas are born, considered, brought into space-time, and where new waking realities are conceived.

For the most part, the following exercises require little explanation, for the concepts have been presented elsewhere. What they do require is a playful, curious, and alert attitude coupled with a real desire to become more of yourself, to let go of your ideas of self-limitations, to embrace the image of a you who is a lot more than body and ego, to become a more aware (and thus responsible) creator of your space-time existence.

Exercise #60

"Games" in this exercise can mean whatever you want it to.

What games do you watch (e.g., on TV) but never play yourself? What games do you play but never or rarely watch? What games attract you but are not in your life? What games do you play and not enjoy?

First, look at the symbolism involved in each game. What is your emotional response to those symbols? What beliefs are behind the emotions?

Experiment with one or all of the games by changing a rule or prop or procedure and then imaginatively experience yourself playing or observing the games under these changed circumstances. Make more changes, do the same thing. See how your responses are affected by the new symbols, examine the beliefs operating.

Invent a game for yourself, either to watch or to play or both. You can use symbols from the previous games or come up with new ones. Make this the most enjoyable game your imagination can conceive of. Don't worry about practicality here—whether the game could actually be pulled off is not a consideration. Create a dream game, the most enjoyable you can come up with.

Now play around with the symbols, props, actions of this game and see what effect that has. If the enjoyment diminishes, let yourself understand this without pondering it. Gradually change this dream until it loses all magic and becomes dull and boring. Then make it distasteful, then frightening. Make it into the most harrowing, disgusting, awful, opposite-of-enjoyable game you can imagine. Stay with the game as long as you can, then totally destroy it.

Now resurrect the enjoyable game and relish every moment of it as you experience it in your imagination.

Exercise #61

Below are some typical space-time sequences of events. The game here is to nip in the bud your "cause-effect" expectations and come up with an event that does not "follow from" the first two but that your imagination associates with them. We do this in dreams all the time, so try it now in waking life. After each sequence below write a short description of "what happens next." The wilder the better. Know that whatever comes to mind will be in some way "relevant." But don't stop to consider how it is relevant until after you've gone down the whole list. Then go back and get in touch with the "felt significance" of each event trio, and look at the beliefs you have attached to it.

1. You are speeding. A cop stops you. Then . . .
2. The telephone rings. You answer it. Then . . .
3. You come into your dark house. You flip the light switch. Then . . .
4. The professor asks a question. You raise your hand. Then . . .
5. You stub your toe. You let out a yell. Then . . .
6. You look out of the airplane window and see its wing break off. You hear the captain's voice over the speaker. Then . . .
7. The dentist picks up his drill. You open your mouth. Then . . .
8. You walk past an expensive restaurant. You see your lover inside lunching with an attractive stranger. Then . . .
9. You take out a cigarette. You flick your Bic. Then . . .
10. You get in line at the post office. You wait. Then . . .
11. Your client makes a bid on the condo. You present the bid to the owner. Then . . .
12. You get a letter from the IRS. You open it. Then . . .
13. You have a headache. You take a pain pill. Then . . .
14. Your mother calls. She asks why you haven't written. Then . . .
15. You have a vivid dream. You tell it to your shrink. Then . . .
16. Your daughter bursts into tears at the dinner table. She says she has something to tell you. Then . . .
17. You arrive home late. Your spouse won't speak to you. Then . . .
18. You reserve tickets for the concert. You go to pick them up. Then . . .
19. You forgot your wallet. The cabbie is waiting. Then . . .
20. A mugger pushes you from behind. You fall down. Then . . .

Exercise #62

According to Seth, when we are born our identity is composed of a variety of "incipient selves." He likens each "self" to a nucleus of an energy gestalt within the psyche, a nucleus that attracts to it a certain proportion of the overall energy available to the identity. This energy has a specific pattern or significance. Translated into space-time terms, one self may be attracted to and draw to it a penchant for history. Another may have a mystical bent. Still another may be strongly paternal. Taken together, these selves are a repository of abilities and interests for the physical personality to draw from.

In some cases the physical self forms a strong personality whose energy so outshadows the energy of any of the incipient selves that it draws them into it where they appear as subsidiary or latent abilities. In other cases, the energy of certain incipient selves will be almost as strong as that of the main personality. If this is the situation they may eventually split apart and go off on their own—into a different system of reality. These are probable selves. To us, theirs is a probable system, not real. To them it is the other way around.

This does not ordinarily happen at birth but after a period of development. For many years we may follow a certain bent and then come to a point when we have to make a choice whether to continue on that path or to take a new one, developing other abilities. Seth told Rob, Jane's husband, a fascinating story. In another system of reality Rob's father had been a well-known inventor using his creative abilities to the fullest and avoiding emotional commitment. Then he met Stella (Rob's mother) and fell deeply in love. At that point he became like two people—"twin nuclei"—with equal but mutually exclusive desires and intents where there was "room" for only one. Thus the personality split into two and one went off into a different system of reality. Neither version of Rob's father was aware of this split, and to each his was the "official" reality.

Most interesting about this story is that both Rob's mother and father had their "strongest" reality in a probable system—probable from our viewpoint, of course. They both developed their abilities to a greater extent in the so-called probable reality than did the selves in *this* reality. From that perspective, Rob's parents were probable selves here. Each of them split off from the "main" personality to explore a path which that personality, preferring to continue to develop already burgeoning abilities, chose not to take. Rob's father, in this reality, chose to marry and to learn more about the emotions, but in the other reality he chose not to marry and to continue with his inventions. His energy in that reality was stronger than in this one, and he developed his chosen abilities to a greater extent.

Sometimes two probable selves who go off to explore two different realities will later in life come back together to once again be part of the same personality in the same reality. And sometimes, after a probable self dies in one reality, its energy will flow back to the remaining self in another reality. Clearly there is a *very close* relationship among probable selves. They are all part of the same psyche and began even as part of the same personality focused within the same system of reality. In that sense, they are *us* and we are *they*.

All the probable selves springing from one personality dream "joint but separate" dreams, in Seth's words—dreams that share the same symbolism, but are viewed from slightly different perspectives, We meet in dreams. We see "what might have been" had we followed a different path and developed other skills. From them we can learn what not to do next time, or what we ought to do. Seth thinks it is now time for us to bring to waking awareness what we nightly discover in dreams about our probable selves and probable realities. He thinks the time is ripe for an expansion of consciousness, of our normal waking consciousness, to tap the wisdom of all those probable selves in those adjacent realities, selves who have explored all of the avenues we haven't here. He says, "The nature of probabilities must be understood, for the time has come in the world as you experience it where the greatest wisdom and discrimination are needed."

This is an exercise, modified to some extent, that Seth suggested in *Unknown Reality* as a means of getting in more conscious touch with our probable selves in other realities. I found when I tried this that it felt dreamlike, and I had a sense of déjà vu, as if I had been there before. Though I couldn't recall specific dreams to explain this, I am quite sure it must have been in dreams that I had visited these other dimensions.

Think of a time in your life when you were faced with a difficult choice. In your imagination follow the scene through to its "official" conclusion— what actually happened. Now imagine what might have been if you had made a different choice. Don't be too intellectual about this. Instead try to *feel* yourself through a probable scenario, going down a different road.

Seth has said that when we get in touch with a probable reality, it has a fuzzy, blurred quality to it, a grayness. And we may feel insubstantial, like a ghost. But if we become thoroughly involved with this exercise, even if we don't have much success with it on a conscious level, Seth says this will begin a "neurological reorientation," eventually making it easier to glimpse realities outside of the one our brains are tuned into. We can come to a point where, anytime we make a decision, we will begin to feel the reality of the opposite decision and its outcome.

He also says our dreams will change. As we get acquainted with probabilities on a conscious level, our dreams will explore them more deeply and vividly than ever before.

Exercise #63

Physical reality can be likened to a plant and nonphysical reality likened to the earth and sky which give it sustenance. The plant draws from the near limitless resources of its environment just those very few elements that it needs at any given time. It draws them into itself and makes them its own. Sunlight and minerals become stems, leaves, flowers—the plant's three-dimensional expression of itself in space-time, an expression as notable for what it is not as for what it is. If the plant is tall and bushy, then it is not simultaneously short and sparse, for space-time does not allow for more than one "identity" at a time. If its flowers are white and sweet-smelling they are not also an odorless red; if the leaves are smooth they are not at the same time prickly. If the plant had believed it possible to have red leaves instead of green, it could have drawn from its environment the resources to create red leaves—or purple or black. Anything the plants "thinks of" and more is out there in the environment for it to make use of. But if the plant chooses red leaves, then it cannot at the same time (and in the same space) have green or purple or black. The agreed-upon rules of space-time will not allow it.

Our habit in space-time, in "making sense" of our environment, of other people, of ourselves, is to focus on physical attributes, on accomplishments, on the ongoing flow of events, our brains serving as data banks for all of the "information" we take in. This information we then use as evidence of who we are and the way the world is. It gives us a space-time blueprint from which to continue creating that reality. Luckily, in our dreams we get a broader perspective, seeing space-time not only for what it is but for what it could be, seeing ourselves not only as who we are officially in space-time but as many other identities (selections of significance) as well. We identify less with "the plant," one possible physical manifestation of selfhood, and more with the "nourishment"—all of the ideas, all of the meanings from which to choose. All of the probable realities.

Take inventory of who you are NOT. Begin by writing down a short physical description of yourself, a list of your talents, activities, and current challenges. Think of each of these as representing a choice you are making, a significance you feel attracted toward. Also take a look at the beliefs you are dealing with.

Now write a list of just a few of the things you are not. Choose those that come immediately to mind, for this indicates a meaningful association of the unchosen attributes with the chosen ones. As you do this the connections may be clear, but if not, don't worry about it. Just list some of the things you are not, some of the activities you are not involved in, some of the challenges not chosen—some of the probable realities you did not choose to manifest.

Now from this second list choose one or a combination of the "paths not taken" that appeal to you and that you wish you could manifest in space-time. If you find yourself thinking, "That's impossible," gently let go of that thought and instead imagine this happening. Summon up as much enthusiasm and zest as you can and playfully picture yourself looking like, being like, acting like this highly probable, very possible self of yours. Feel with that self, be that self. Really identify with that feeling.

As Seth has said, experience is knowledge. By experiencing yourself as this person you'd like to be, you are picking up on the knowledge of how to be him or her, of how that being feels. This is bound to make a difference in your reality. Be open to unexpected results. Remember that any meaning/significance/essence can appear in space-time in a multitude of guises, so don't look so much for an envisioned form to manifest itself as for a felt, now familiar, significance to become part of your space-time experience.

Try to get in the habit of seeing and thinking beyond "what is" in space-time to "what could be." Our space-time habits of viewing our present reality as the only possible one slows down our growth, for we can only accept small changes along the way instead of accepting large, dramatic new creations.

Exercise #64

Immersing ourselves imaginatively in waking dreams is one of the best ways to expand consciousness and to familiarize ego consciousness with the nature and scope of dreaming consciousness—as you have probably discovered from the waking dream exercises so far in this book. There will be several more in this chapter.

Seth often used a playwright analogy to describe our true role in creating our reality. Far from being mere actors on the stage of life with given lines and prescribed actions, we are both the actors in and the creators of our dramas. But the "writing" is an ongoing process, based on a very flexible blueprint; the actors are always free to improvise and interpret and change the whole direction of the play, "killing off" old characters, introducing new, adding more acts, and providing different settings and props. We tend to lose awareness of our "writer" role as we act and tend to believe we haven't much choice as to how to perform our role. In fact, we forget it is a play we are in and believe the stage, the props, the characters are "the real world."

With this in mind, write a waking dream-play. See yourself behind the scenes as the writer/observer/director advising and commenting as the drama unfolds. Participate in turn with each of the actors in the play, all of whom are aware of their power within the play to make it what they want, who are aware, too, that they are not their roles, but have playfully agreed to take them on for what they could learn from them. Write the dream as you imagine it unfolding, as you imagine the play within the dream taking its course. Savor the feeling of being so creative, of knowing you have total free choice in how your play turns out.

Exercise #65

In *Psyche* Seth proposes a number of consciousness-stretching exercises, designed both to acquaint us with the way dream consciousness operates (and thus give us a sense of trusting familiarity when in the dream state) and to show us through our own experiencing of it that we can direct our waking consciousness in ways we may not have realized. These exercises will be interspersed throughout this chapter.

This first exercise asks you to stretch your time conception. Begin by working with objects that go through familiar cyclical changes. Trees, for example. Look at the trees in your neighborhood and perceive them in a different season. If it is spring, picture them in the fall; if it's winter, envision them in summer. Look at them, see them, make them real now, as they exist in a different time. Once you can do this easily, then choose a given tree and see it in all of its seasons, in fall, in winter, spring, summer. View it, not just as this tree at this time, but as treeness throughout time, as a lasting significance transcending the yearly seasons. Look at other trees, flowers, all beings of nature in this way. Get in the habit of viewing them from this widened time perspective, not as objects in time but as both a stage in a process and the process itself. Feel that process within you and begin to tune into yourself and your loved ones in this way—not as beings fixed within a certain location and time slot but as an ongoing process, as much more than who we are "right now." See yourself and others as what you were and what you will be. See yourself and them and all of your surroundings from this "larger" perspective.

Exercise #66

Exercise your imagination by writing for yourself a fairy tale—or science fiction story or fantasy or similar fictional story. The only rule is that the characters and/or the actions be "unreal" in a few or a number of ways. Something that "couldn't happen" in normal life. Be playful, have fun, and create your work of fiction. If you find that the physical act of writing something down interferes with the creative process, try tape recording it, but do somehow get the original words recorded.

The next day, analyze and interpret your story as if it were a dream, playing with it in many of the ways you have done so far in this book. Take note of its parallels with dreams (both waking and sleeping ones), and look for some differences. Since in this exercise you used your consciousness a little differently from the way you do in regular dreams or waking dreams, you can expect to find some new images, new beliefs, and new significances to add to your growing self-knowledge.

Exercise #67

Go back through the exercises you have done so far and make a list of the symbols you have come up with, which you have encountered in your dreams, imaginings, and creative play.

1. Look at your list of symbols and let one attract you to it. Write it down or draw it on another piece of paper. Write or draw around it all the events you associate with it through your feeling of significance. Describe or draw colors, objects, sounds, emotions, qualities, thoughts—everything you associate with that symbol.
2. Go through this same process with several symbols from the list, using a different piece of paper for each one.
3. Now compare your collection. See how many symbols you can find that occur on every page, that you associated with each original symbol. Write these on another page.
4. Now look at these. Instead of adding to this group through associations, see if you can reduce these symbols to one that contains all of them. It could be that one of the symbols you already have there feels to you as if it includes the others, or it may be that you need another symbol within which those on this page will "fit." In your imagination, see those symbols before you lose their form. See a single new symbol appear that in some felt way reflects to you the meaning of all of them.
5. Now look back at your collection of associated symbols. Extract from each page the original symbol and write it or draw it on the same page with the symbol from #4. See if you can also "subsume" these old symbols under your new symbol. Does it feel as if these original symbols you chose from the list and which you associated with a number of others, does it feel as if these too can fit within the felt meaning context of the new symbol?

The idea here is to come up with one powerful significance-filled symbol that transcends opposites, unites polarities. But don't force it. If it doesn't come to you here, ask for it in a dream. If nothing comes to you, that's okay. You've still learned a lot more about yourself from doing this exercise.

But if you do come up with such a symbol, you can use it in times of stress, use its strongly felt significance to reassure you of the basic connectedness of all space-time phenomena.

Exercise #68

As Seth has said many times, there are no divisions to our consciousness. The dream state and the waking state are not two mutually exclusive portions of our awareness, but different focuses we take for different purposes. In dreams we work out challenges encountered in waking life; in waking life we work through challenges we set up for ourselves in dreams. When we sleep, the waking dimension of our consciousness continues to operate and we are peripherally aware of what is going on with our bodies and surroundings in space-time. You saw this in the last chapter, where within the dream state you "looked in on" the waking state, experiencing it as dreamlike. So too, when we are awake, the sleeping dimension of consciousness continues to operate and we are peripherally aware of what is going on in that dimension.

In this exercise, sit down, relax, and become aware of the peripheral world of dreams that exists simultaneously with waking reality. View it in much the same fashion as you did in the exercise of the last chapter where you looked in on waking reality while asleep. Don't attempt to take on a dreaming state of consciousness, but simply become aware of that active world of dreams happening concurrently with space-time. Get a sense of how dreams support and supplement your waking reality, how your everyday occurrences are paralleled in some manner within dreams. Sense the underlying dream reality interacting with waking reality, the feedback between the two flowing back and forth. Feel how inextricably connected the two states of consciousness are.

Once you have done this exercise and experienced the feeling of being a part of two realities at once, the one (dreaming) peripheral, the other (waking) central, you should be able fairly easily to regain this perception whenever you decide to summon it up. You can "check in with dreaming reality" anytime to see what is going on there, how it parallels what is happening in space-time, how it supports and nourishes your waking existence. This will increase your sense of wholeness and unity, your sense of rootedness within a "larger" reality.

Exercise #69

Seth has said that what we experience in dreams is more real than what we experience in waking reality. Within dreams, consciousness is more fluid and far-ranging, reflecting at least to some extent the qualities of the pure, undivided, unfocused consciousness out of which all realities are created. Space-time is a highly specialized learning ground for discovering on a minute scale and in great detail how and why our focus and feelings create the realities that they do. The rules of waking reality require a portion of the consciousness participating in it to become "solidified" into shape and duration within time and space, and another portion to "sense" that shape and duration. Consciousness must be drastically "held in" and constricted in order to carry this off. The result is a most interesting (and, according to Seth, to many of its "outside observers" a very dear) reality. Space-time reality could usefully be viewed as a snapshot taken by a camera that, at the time it snaps the picture, arbitrarily gives shapes to the constantly shifting energy of which it is a part, creating images where before there was process, and puts these on a screen where consciousness can get a look at what "before" would not have been noticeable. The photo does not show consciousness as it "really" is, but rather it symbolizes conscious processes.

We have seen in many of the preceding exercises how richly symbolic our waking life is and what it can tell us of our own consciousness. This exercise, with a slightly different approach from the others, offers yet another new and uncharacteristic glimpse into space-time. Seth has suggested this exercise, and so has Sue Watkins in her latest book. She said that it would be enlightening. I want to share with you what happened with me as I did this exercise.

The instructions themselves are simple: Write down a recent event *as if* it were a dream and then interpret it. That "as if" is important, for in making the decision to recall the event as a dream, you provide yourself with an entirely different experiencing of it. As I wrote down what follows, I was surprised that, at the time I was experiencing the events of that day, their symbolic quality largely escaped me. Though certainly not entirely: I was especially aware of a nostalgic, almost déjà vu, feeling underlying all others as things happened around me and to me. The instant I began writing, that dreamlike nostalgia took precedence over all the events, which became secondary to their felt meaning. Here goes (again, names are changed to preserve privacy).

A Recent Event AS IF It Were a Dream (8/2/88)

I am with Bill and we are at a Sunday afternoon party by a pool. A huge rundown cabana flanks one side. It is in 1940s art-deco style with much ornate, wrought-iron furniture, white paint chipping off, rattan chairs in need of a new finish, new cushions. The atmosphere is nostalgic—faded. This was once Lana Turner's estate and it feels as if the ghosts of movie stars linger here.

A large bar along the back, a sculptured wrought-iron chrysanthemum above, dressing rooms on either side—"ladies" and "men." Many tables and chairs, enough for a very large party. You can almost hear the champagne corks pop.

I am the only woman at the party. The rest are all gay young men. Bill, at forty, is the second-oldest person here next to me.

The pool is gigantic and deep with many leaves in it from the profusion of trees on the green lawn across from us. At one end a double cement staircase goes up two flights. Between the two sets of stairs is a waterslide flanked by cactus plants. It reminds me of the Alhambra somehow, with its fountain-lined balustrades.

Bill and I are at the top of the slide looking down. From above it looks a long, steep way down that slide to the blue pool below. He urges me to go down the slide. I had thought I wanted to but now I hesitate. No, not now. The young men laugh and giggle as they repeatedly slide down into the pool, some backwards, some sitting up facing forward, others lying down, two toboggan-style. Bill slides down on an air mattress. I finally go down too. And then again. And again.

Some women arrive, stay a moment, leave. A trendy-looking couple come, offer me some of the fine wine they brought, some of their bagel chips and Camembert. They are partners in a new and fabulously popular restaurant, he the cook/artist, she the business manager. We talk of the relativity of age while Bill sits off by himself, withdrawn.

As soon as I wrote the "dream" down, I reread it and was struck by how selective I had been in my description. I had been fairly thorough in describing the cabana and other physical surroundings, but many of the events I had left out, and of the many people there, focused on only three besides myself. I could certainly remember those other events and those other people, but when I looked upon the Sunday happening as a dream, particular details stood out from the others. I realized it was the same way with actual dreams: Certain details sprang out at me from amidst others, attracted me to them (or them to me) through their significance. Our ordinary memory is selective too, choosing significant events over others to remember, but it would seem that when in a more dreamy mode our significance-selecting apparatus is more acute and sensitive.

I put this aside at that point, and the next day returned to it, interpreting it in much the same way I had my dreams—except in this case I looked to my dreams rather than to waking life to find parallel symbols to use in my analysis. What I wrote is much too long to repeat here (and parts are too embarrassingly personal), but in the passage below you can see how I got the analysis going, setting up a lot of ideas/symbols to later take a look at. I did later zero in on some and really learned a lot about some old beliefs I was still carrying around, and about some new challenges ahead. Anyway, this may give you some ideas as to how to proceed with your own analysis.

What Bill represents: playful, impish, spontaneous, artistic, close—can talk about anything, the "artistic temperament." The setting: 1940s high school, college days, swing, pool parties, Lana Turner, innocence or . . . what? . . . a lot less consciousness . . . lower level of consciousness, a more conventional time as compared to now, lacking in enlightenment . . . a darkness and decadence . . . decadence, decaying culture (more so than now?) . . . nostalgia . . . unreal . . . like a dream, the 1940s when I passed from adolescent to adult, ten to twenty years old . . . was in Palo Alto most of that time . . . of course, the *war!* . . . not much impact on me, the war, despite living in early 1940s in Seattle where Boeing shipyards turned out a ship a day and my fourteen-year-old brother made megabucks working there . . . father in Alaska. All I thought about was boys and how to be popular—going to Palo Alto a shock, so sophisticated. But, looking back, it feels like it's packed with wool . . . what am I trying to say? Cotton batting. Stuffed all around, keeping out the rest of the world.

Is that the way *now* feels? Here? Well, the sea does shut out other sounds, even provides its own breezes so that the prevailing weather, much hotter, doesn't come in. My own little world, no TV, no one around, unseeable from the sea, my own little island unto itself.

So, am I likening this time in my life to *that* time? In other ways? In the 1950s I came into the adult world . . . working, putting husband through law school, having a child, learning to be an adult (and balking the whole time). But 1940s. The war and all but I hardly knew that was going on . . . just interested in my appearance, being popular . . . the setting Sunday evoked with nostalgia the 1940s, which, despite the war years, was romantic and unreal (as compared to 1950s, for example), a time to posture about and to play. Many of the young men at the party were in their late teens, as I was then, and they were acting now that I think of it very much like we did in the 1940s, posturing and playing. Gay in the old sense of the word. And that they were gay rather than heterosexual, too, fits in with the 1940s theme, for my sexuality then (as I later came to know it) lay dormant. Hmmm, much to explore here. The slide itself has significance on all kinds of levels from risk and the unknown and plunging into the sea of life to letting go to allowing pleasure to giving up "control." Hmmm. And then there's the restaurant couple, who brought me back to "now" and gave me another look at my attraction and ambivalence toward partnership and toward art/business combined and, yes, age, and the relativity thereof. Much to ponder here.

Exercise #70

No doubt about it, the "as if a dream" perspective on waking life brings to conscious awareness a lot of underlying feelings and beliefs that might ordinarily escape our notice. In addition, taking this perspective shows us once again that we can switch to a different state of consciousness through our desire to do so—and each time we discover this, the easier it gets. Also, the "as if" exercise shows us very clearly how inextricably related dream reality and waking reality are, growing out of and reinforcing one another, each symbolizing the other. Since this perspective has so many benefits, I'm presenting two more exercises here that show other ways you can practice taking this view of waking reality.

Try taking the "as if" perspective with an unresolved conflict in your life. View that conflict, the circumstances around it, the people involved, as if you were dreaming about it. Write down or tape-record this dream perspective and become familiar with the meaning of the symbols, and with the underlying feelings and beliefs.

Now continue the dream and bring it to a satisfying conclusion. In the last chapter you did this with "real" dreams. Here, create a waking dream that continues where you left off, that begins with the challenge in its dream trappings and carries it to a felt conclusion, to where you feel the conflict is resolved emotionally.

You can add to the power of this process by suggesting that you dream about the challenge as well and work through it in the regular dream state.

Exercise #71

Tam Mossman, who for years was Jane Roberts's editor at Prentice Hall and who in the process became thoroughly versed in the Seth material, made it a habit to view ordinary objects around him as highly symbolic representations of his own feelings and beliefs. A "specialty" of his was trash. As he walked the streets of his native Philadelphia, he made it a point to observe what trash he saw along the way. His attitude was that each piece of it had a message for him, that it was no accident he happened to pass by any such item, that it was in his life, if briefly, for a purpose, to tell him something about himself. He said that when he took this perspective, such things as discarded whiskey bottles or old shoes, or any number of common everyday objects he would scarcely notice ordinarily, all of a sudden took on meaning for him much as such "props" do in dreams. Suddenly these items were not just whiskey bottles or shoes, but instead a commentary on his feelings and beliefs at the time. If he was worried about something, sure enough he'd come across a piece of trash which in some way symbolized that worry for him, often in surprising ways that gave him new insights into the worry, gave him a new perspective on it, new nuances to consider.

What Mossman was doing, in effect, was looking at a certain aspect of waking reality as if it were a dream, assuming that every object he encountered had an underlying significance. He well knew that nothing "enters" space-time that is not of strong meaning to us, created in order to show us how our most compelling ideas look when materialized.

Begin to notice the objects you surround yourself with, the ones you "accidentally" encounter on your way from a to b, items you choose to buy, things your friends happen to have in their homes when you visit. Take note of them, feel them resonating with significance, realize they were created by you for some reason. There is a message in each of them, something to learn this very instant about your worldview. In many cases you will already know what they mean to you, but in those "accidental" or puzzling cases you can gain from taking a minute or two to associate the object with others, with feelings you have, with what is going on in your life, and of course, to recent dream material. Use the props you have created for yourself to the best of your advantage: to grow and learn from here in space-time. Let the consciousness you are familiar with in the dream state enter into waking life and help you make sense of your life through showing you its meaning as contained in its every object.

Exercise #72

This is another consciousness-stretching exercise Seth proposed in order to get us to use our waking consciousness in unaccustomed ways, making it easier for us to be "awake" within the dream state, and familiarizing us with the way dream awareness operates.

As you're walking along the sidewalk or driving down the road or sitting outside in the sun, project your consciousness high above your head and look down on yourself from that bird's-eye viewpoint. Do this playfully and see how it feels to be at the same time the you down below and also a you looking down. The whole idea here is to enjoy this stretching of your consciousness. Every now and again, when you think of it, stretch your consciousness in this way.

Exercise #73

In a previous exercise you created your own fairy tale, or "bedtime story." In this exercise begin with a bedtime story you like, and "translate" it into waking life. As you did with dream interpretation, first decide what each character in the tale represents to you, how the events of the story reflect inner concerns of yours, what the objects mean. Then write a real-life version of the tale in which you figure as a prominent (if not leading) character. While sticking to the theme of the story, try to write a true-to-life scenario, something that could plausibly happen within your own life.

Exercise #74

Now try doing the opposite. We all have "stories" to tell our friends about certain episodes in our life where we may have met a challenge successfully after some adversity, or had a memorable encounter or series of encounters with someone, or taken a trip, or had what we'd call an adventure. Choose one of these stories and translate it into a tale of the supernatural. Really exaggerate and have fun with it. Pull out all the stops. See how talented you can be in recounting your heroic deeds.

Exercise #75

Next time you become aware of an irrelevant thought "crossing" your mind, take off and follow it. (That is, unless you are executing a turn in your car, lecturing before a class, or engaging in other such attention-demanding activities.) Follow it and see where it goes. It could lead you into some mental territory that turns out to be most relevant to your life at this point in time.

Exercise #76

Here are some space-time actions. "Translate" each one into an equivalent space-time action, an action with roughly the same felt meaning to it, about which you feel pretty much the same way. Write your response after each listing.

1. Shampooing your hair _____
2. Dancing alone by yourself _____
3. Paying taxes _____
4. Smoking a joint _____
5. Slipping on a wet floor _____
6. Buying a birthday present for a child _____
7. Boarding an airplane _____
8. Diapering a baby _____
9. Answering a letter from a friend _____
10. Swimming in the ocean _____.
11. Doing the laundry _____
12. Kissing your mate _____
13. Kissing your child _____
14. Kissing your parent _____
15. Kissing a friend _____
16. Driving in traffic _____
17. Eating a salad _____
18. Getting money from the bank _____
19. Locking your house _____
20. Watching football _____
21. Drinking beer _____
22. Calling from a pay phone _____
23. Playing drums _____
24. Waiting in line _____
25. Ordering a pizza _____
26. Jogging _____
27. Watching the news _____
28. Sawing a board _____
29. Cheering the team _____
30. Singing "The Star-Spangled Banner" _____
31. Visiting a sick friend _____
32. Taking your boat out _____
33. Buying a house _____

34. Hiking _____
35. Going to Europe _____
36. Coming on to someone _____
37. Letting someone come on to you _____
38. Calling the police _____
39. Getting a new credit card _____
40. Fasting for a day _____
41. Parking the car in a tight space _____
42. Christmas shopping _____
43. Asking for a loan _____
44. Flunking your driver's test _____
45. Target practice _____
46. Cooking Thanksgiving dinner _____
47. Having someone cook Thanksgiving dinner for you _____
48. Breaking up with someone _____
49. Getting books out of the library _____
50. Losing at Trivial Pursuit _____

Now go back down the list, and this time after each pair of actions put down a dream action or some other symbol that feels roughly equivalent to the two actions. Imagine how your dreaming consciousness would symbolize the meanings and feelings contained within the two space-time actions. Write down what comes to mind. When you are through doing that, go down the list and take note of those items you reacted to with strong feelings, either positive or negative. For these items, come up with some other symbols, both from space-time and dreams, that also represent that feeling and meaning. And/or look back through your imagination and dream exercises for symbols that would fit on this list of strongly meaningful material.

Exercise #77

Get some clay and sculpt your feelings and beliefs.

Exercise #78

Seth has said that what we think of as impulses are often messages from forgotten dreams. Even though we didn't remember the dream, a fragment of it came to our conscious mind for our use in space-time. Impulses are an attention signal, something like the tip of an iceberg, telling us there is a meaningful dream waiting for us just beneath the surface. Certainly it behooves us to pay attention to our impulses, for they're bound to have a helpful message for us in space-time. They bring two messages, really, the impulse itself being one message, and the dream eliciting the impulse (if we can uncover the dream) being another. The first message tells us what to do, the second, why. And, though we all know it isn't necessary or even possible to always know why we do something (or don't), understanding our reasons gives us a sense of confidence and security. Thus it may be worth our effort to try to uncover the dream out of which the impulse arose.

The first step is to become aware of your impulses, whether or not you follow them. (Sue Watkins, as she relates in her latest book, decided she was going to take note of *and act upon* her impulses, and found this led to all sorts of emotional revelations, many of which were far from pleasant, to say the least. So, be forewarned about a determination to follow your impulses. Though Sue was ultimately glad she had done this, she had a rough time of it for a while.) If you aren't aware of impulses coming to you, it isn't because there aren't any but because you may have one of the following beliefs about them:

1. That impulses are of a base nature, "animal instincts" that must be repressed
2. That you should live your life "rationally" (and since you believe impulses to be "irrational," you ignore them)
3. That if you're aware of an impulse, you have to follow it, and this would be too distracting or time-consuming or something else (so you pretend not to notice it)

If one of the above beliefs fits, playfully exaggerate it out of all proportion to the point where it seems ridiculous and unbelievable. Or tell yourself you are going to pretend you have the opposite belief and then go ahead and pretend. Or make a tape to listen to when going to sleep that suggests a belief favoring impulses and reassuring you that remembering them is perfectly okay.

When impulses come to you, write them down instantly. Then work with them as if they were a fragment of a dream. Seek their symbolic meaning. Seek symbols that represent the impulse. In every way try to extend the meaning.

Keep your mind open and receptive to images, and when they come, write a description of them. Assume they are additional fragments from the same dream, and interpret them with that in mind. Make associations to the impulse, associate the images with one another. Eventually you should have a series of scenes. Now, with your mind in much the state of consciousness you use to create waking and "as if" dreams, put together a dream using the pieces you have collected. You will know you have succeeded when you have that aha feeling, when you understand (whether or not you can articulate it) why the impulse came to you. You'll see the background out of which it arose, you'll see it in context, you'll see the whole gestalt.

Exercise #79

As already noted (in Exercise #64), Seth has said that we have the ability (and present need) to tune in to and learn from the experiences of our probable selves and probable realities. In the previous exercise on probable selves, the goal was to follow a "path not taken" and thereby get in touch with a probable self on that path.

In this exercise you will visit a series of probable realities. This time the goal will be, rather than tuning in to one individual in one reality, to get a sense of probable reality systems as a whole—how they operate, their achievements and challenges, the overall emotional atmosphere.

Begin by making two columns on a piece of paper and labeling them "Positive" and "Negative." Now list widespread phenomena in our society you consider to fit under one category or the other. These may pertain to attitudes or practices in relation to the body and health, family and children, the environment, ways of governing, morality, power, God, something else. Look over the lists and choose some items from each category you want to focus on.

For each item, the idea is to imagine yourself actively immersed in a world where this phenomenon is entirely different. Some obvious examples would be a world without wars of any kind, a world without money, a world without disease or illness, a world without marriage and family, or a world without a moral code. You need not necessarily come up with an *opposite* phenomenon, but with a world in which the attitudes and practices in that regard would seem foreign to us.

Be sure to use items from both categories. Your tendency might be to choose more "negative" items, and to visualize worlds in which the opposite is true. But you can learn at least as much by envisioning worlds in which our positive attributes do not exist, or come across as negative.

Feeling is important here. As you immerse yourself in the world, temporarily let go of your identity in this reality as much as possible and take on the beliefs of that reality. Notice the results of those beliefs; especially notice how you feel with them. You may be surprised, when immersing yourself in a different belief system, that it feels much different from the expected—indicating some beliefs of your own you weren't aware of.

Of course, right here in this world of ours we can find areas without war, areas where people don't use money, and so on. It goes without saying that it is possible (and common) to live in this world without subscribing to all of its mass beliefs. Still, there has got to be a big difference between living in a world whose prevailing belief system promotes competition and living in a world promoting cooperation—despite one's individual belief system. And those differences are what this exercise explores.

Exercise #80

We tend to identify ourselves exclusively with our bodies, seeing them as "us," everything outside them being "not us." It is our bodies that afford us the sensations of sight, sound, touch, smell, taste. But we don't think of it in those terms, we don't think "the body" affords "us" those sensations, rather we think it is "we-the-body" who tastes, smells, touches, and so on. It rarely if ever occurs to us that the body itself has its own sense of identification and its own ways of sensing—its own mode of consciousness. And that which we identify as "us" is really a mode of consciousness operating simultaneously with body consciousness but for the most part with little awareness of it. It is true that our bodies are a very important part of our identities and that to know ourselves means to know that aspect of ourselves. But so long as we focus in on the body as a physical mechanism and ignore the consciousness that keeps it in a state of constant creation, we cannot be said to know the body.

A common misconception is that consciousness—our consciousness, what we identify as us—resides within the brain, which also controls bodily functions. In this image there is no "room" for two aware consciousnesses to exist, for one brain simultaneously to "be" the ego and also the body. And, since it seems to us that via the brain we are aware of ourselves as us and not as cells and organs and the like, we assume aware-of-self consciousness does not exist within the body.

The brain's main function is to be a timing mechanism, regulating the flow of energy and thus information from nonmaterial to material reality. As such it services both ego consciousness and body consciousness but is the "seat" of neither. Both modes of consciousness have their greater existence in nonphysical reality, unconstrained by time and space, free to roam and explore. In fact, body consciousness has much "more" of its existence in nonphysical reality than does ego consciousness, leaving it up to the ego to decide what is of greatest significance in space-time and then joyfully form matter out of it. In this sense the body is more aware than the ego, more in touch with the context out of which space-time arises. As Seth has said, we have much to learn from our body and its "natural knowing."

Sit down in a quiet place, relax, close your eyes, and let your consciousness go within and join with the consciousness of the cells. Tune in to the hum of the cells, to their simultaneous perceptions, to their ahas as they know without thinking, feel without believing. Become cellular consciousness, simultaneously aware of itself as an entity and of itself as all of consciousness, knowing itself in the deep stillness of mind. Feel this part of yourself, this portion of your consciousness that creates your body, your consciousness in this mode as body-creator. Feel its vitality, its exuberance; feel its security and serenity and trust. Tune in to this very familiar, very intimate, very dear form of yourself.

Exercise #81

According to Seth TV is like a "mass shared dream." It reflects our beliefs on a mass level, and through its many dramas we experience and mull over probable realities for ourselves and for society. From this viewpoint, we not only create it but it creates us, and since this is so, we can learn a lot about the "influences" at work there by taking a fresh look at TV fare.

One way is simply to become aware, when viewing your usual programs, what beliefs are being dramatized. Ask yourself whether these are beliefs you agree with, ones you would like to have, or ones you definitely are not interested in ascribing to. Just by being aware of the mostly unstated assumptions of the TV characters you can prevent yourself from falling into the habit of thinking the same way—if you don't want to think that way. Or, if you particularly admire a character and his or her beliefs, you can actively affirm them and practice them in your own life.

Another way is to "visit" the many shows you don't ordinarily view, to really get an idea of what a large number of people think or are trying out. You may find you have a lot more in common with these points of view than you realized. Take a look at the ideas and symbols you feel attracted to and examine the beliefs behind them. Decide whether or not you want the reality implied by those beliefs. Decide whether or not you'll choose to incorporate them in your own worldview.

Exercise #82

Write a waking dream in which you are an animal. To get yourself in the mind frame for this, you may want to look back at some of your dreams for animal (or part-animal) characters that have appeared in them, and in your imagination become one of those, generating the waking dream from there. Or you might choose a space-time animal you identify with strongly and go into the dream as this animal. Create the dream, then interpret it as usual. You could come up with some new insights and areas of significance.

Exercise #83

In this consciousness-stretching exercise, expand yourself adjacently. Let your consciousness of self expand so that it includes, as part of you, your surroundings. Expand and expand, filling up adjacent space. Feel yourself filling that space, part of that space.

Exercise #84

Seth's material on sexuality in *Psyche* is a marvelous antidote to *Playboy* and *Cosmopolitan*—or for that matter, *Good Housekeeping* and *Field and Stream*. The media reflect back, reinforce, and perpetuate our prevailing social belief that men and women are very different from one another. The male is seen as being aggressive, active, logical-minded, inventive, outwardly oriented, a builder of civilizations; the female is perceived as being passive, intuitive, nurturing, creative, concerned with preserving the status quo, disliking change. It is true that feminist literature has made some inroads with these stereotypes, at least for that of the female, but not as much as one would think, especially if you take a look at a magazine like *New Woman*. The basic assumption still seems to be that men and women are inherently different from one another, psychologically as well as physically. Believing this, we create that reality for ourselves, bringing up our children to mirror the psychological traits we believe are appropriate to their sex. Those who cannot or will not at least minimally ascribe to the prevalent belief system in this area most often have a rough time of it, feeling guilty, unattractive, angry or depressed, defensive, rejected.

Seth says we put far too much emphasis on sexual roles and not nearly enough on individuality; that we are individuals first and foremost. Mankind chose a particular biological orientation as a means to continue the species, but no specific psychological attributes are necessarily connected to biological function. In fact, if males were truly as aggressive as we believe them to be, the cooperation necessary for survival would have been impossible, and the race would have perished long ago. Our "caveman" stereotype is not at all reflective of the way it really was. Cave dwellers were democratic, sharing "masculine" and "feminine" tasks equally. Modern men and women in that sense are far less "civilized" than used to be the case.

There is no such thing as a male psyche or a female psyche. Our larger personhood is male and female, which means each of us focused in space-time is basically bisexual. It is this bisexual nature that ensures the necessary cooperation for physical survival and cultural interaction. And it is this bisexual nature that is expressed and reflected in homosexual relationships, just as it is expressed through heterosexual relationships. There is nothing unnatural in bisexuality; it is our natural bent and frees us to express all the facets of our own individual being.

Our dreams clearly reflect our bisexual nature, where we encounter androgynous beings, or characters who change from one sex to the other before our eyes, where "we" as the main character find ourselves to be of the opposite sex from our space-time orientation. Since dreams mirror the contents of our psyches, how could a psyche that was "basically female" or "basically male" contain such images? Bisexuality is a basic fact of our being, and accepting that frees us to express ourselves fully in space-time, to use our creativity to the fullest.

Just as the word "sex" tends to evoke physical imagery, so too does the term "bisexual," which is enough to scare some of us off immediately (while affording others with a sense of relief). Though Seth says that a person's having physical relations with both male and female is a natural expression of bisexuality, it is by no means the only one. In fact, it is a small part of bisexual expression. More important and far-reaching are our psychological acceptance and encouragement of all traits within us, whether "masculine" or "feminine."

Because the Western world is currently reexamining sexual roles, many of us find ourselves rebelling against the stereotypes of ourselves we used to accept and, instead, emphasize their opposite. Tired of being stereotyped as intuitive, women show how very rational and "tough-minded" they can be. Men, disliking the macho image, deny their assertive qualities and become passive. And so we trade one set of stereotypes for another and deny one half of our being while embracing the other half.

To what degree (through actions, thoughts, feelings) do you accept and encourage the following traits within yourself, within your mate, your children, your friends? Which ones do you discourage?

1. *Aggressive* (assert yourself, go for it, do it)
2. *Active* (exercise, work, hike, bike, use your mind, don't vegetate)
3. *Logical-minded* (figure it out, analyze it, weigh the pros and cons, be rational)
4. *Inventive* (make it, change it, switch things around)
5. *Outwardly oriented* (what you see is what you get, what will people think, how can I help the world)
6. *Builder of civilizations* (go into politics, fight for a cause, make war, make peace, liberal)
7. *Passive* (laid-back, unargumentative, receptive, wimpy, come what may, uninvolved, in your own world)
8. *Intuitive* (spiritual, irrational, naturally wise, flaky)
9. *Creative* (full of ideas, artistic, unpredictable, difficult)
10. *Nurturing* (compassionate, helpful, selfless, service-oriented)
11. *Status-quo preserver* (conservative, good enough, contented, smug)
12. *Dislike change* (security oriented, timid, patriotic, fixed)

In your imagination, take on those traits you do NOT accept and encourage within yourself. Really get into the part and experience those attributes, see how they feel. If they feel good, consider developing them; if not, look at your beliefs in that area. You may find that your beliefs are standing in the way of developing some true potentials for yourself.

Now, in your imagination, become a member of the opposite sex, but remain "yourself." In what way does having a different physical orientation influence your feelings about yourself? Is it okay for you to be you and have this different body? Does having this different body allow you to behave in ways you can't ordinarily? Why?

Ask your dreams to guide you in developing all of your potential, to accept your individuality and uniqueness.

Exercise #85

Words often get in the way of our perceptions and feelings. We look at a rock, we think "rock," and we dismiss it. "Just another rock." So the qualities of rockness, the meaning behind rocks, what they symbolize, escape us, not to mention the individuality of that particular rock—how the sunshine plays across it, its texture and color, its shape and position, how it stands out from its background—the quality of its consciousness.

In this exercise, go out into nature, find a tree or a rock or a stream and merge your consciousness with that natural entity. Imagine yourself within and composed of that being, that configuration of consciousness expressing itself symbolically through treeness, rockness, streamness. Become that being, feel as that being, perceive as that being.

Doing this exercise successfully just once will forever alter the way you see your world.

Exercise #86

Words do often get in the way of our perceptions and feelings. In this exercise, give new names to common objects around you. Use "nonsense" syllables that convey your felt sense of the object. Play with the sounds, take pleasure in the way they trip off your tongue, pay attention to what they evoke. Feel for the sounds that unite images and feelings and object.

Write a "nonsense" poem whose meaning is the sounds of its words, the way it looks on the page. Have fun.

Exercise #87

Look around you, let an object attract you, and give it a different name, using a "real" word that traditionally stands for a concrete object. For instance, call the couch a turtle. Whatever concrete noun comes first to mind, use that, then see how it affects your perception of the object, how that object changes in your perceptions and takes on new characteristics.

Name another object and see how this again changes your perceptions slightly, how the two newly named objects change your feelings about your environment. Continue doing this, and as you do so, visualize the objects becoming what you named them—the couch becoming a turtle, and so on. See how that feels. Then change the names to something abstract—truth, fidelity, patience, fun. See what this does to your perceptions. Feel the power, and limitations, of words.

Exercise #88

In the previous chapter you brought about flying dreams for yourself. In this exercise, create a flying dream in the waking state. Write a waking dream in which you leave your body and take off flying, free of spatial and temporal constraints, free to transport yourself instantly to anyplace you want to go, to look in on friends, check out other parts of the world. Later, compare it with your usual flying dreams.

Exercise #89

Another consciousness-stretcher: Perceive yourself and the world as it will exist fifty years from now. Look around the neighborhood and sense it as it will be in fifty years. Look at people and see them as they will look then, what clothes they will be wearing, cars they will be driving. How will your work have changed in fifty years? Your children? The world in general? Sense the most likely probable future for yourself.

Exercise #90

Reincarnation is a topic of abiding interest, attracting its skeptics, detractors, true believers, and lately, therapists—who hypnotically "regress" their clients to a "previous" life, where they get a new perspective on this one. All too often I hear people excusing their present problems in terms of something they did in a past life. The term "karma" often enters in this discussion, the idea that, as Shirley MacLaine puts it, "what goes around comes around." Too often the idea of karma, sound in itself, is misconstrued to mean "I don't really create my own reality. I am at the mercy of my past—my far distant past of several lifetimes ago—when I did thus-and-so and am paying for it now." Seth warns his readers about taking on this attitude and thus giving up our power (and responsibility) in the present to form our lives.

Once again—and I wonder if this can ever be said enough—in the world of probable events where our space-time reality originates, space and time do not exist. What we conceive of as past, present, and future is energy/consciousness existing now, happening now, in the Spacious Present, as Seth calls it. Just as our actions in this lifetime influence and change both our past and future, so too do they influence previous and future *selves*. And so do the actions of previous and future selves influence us. We are all in this together, learning from one another the wonder and power of consciousness.

Thus, it makes just as much sense to say that a previous version of yourself has taken on a karmic debt because of your "misdeeds" in this lifetime. Or that a future self has "caused you" to act in a certain way through its mistaken ideas. It's known as buck passing, and though it may be tempting to take such a stance, ultimately it's debilitating, insofar as we lose our sense of power in the now to create our reality.

What goes around does come around, for this is a natural outcome of our explorations of significance. We cannot possibly understand the significance of, say, rape, without being both the perpetrator and the victim, both the passive bystander and outraged parent. When we set out to explore meaning, we explore meaning.

But, because even the "smallest" area of significance has infinite facets to it, no physical being can in his or her allotted space and time possibly explore them all. That is why the reincarnational system exists, as well as the probability systems and the counterpart system.

We have seen that probability systems explore alternate actions, different nuances, and other paths, in a different but parallel system of reality. The reincarnational system differs from the probability systems in that the entities involved are in the same system of reality but in different time slots (which of course do not exist in nonphysical reality: Our reincarnational selves, like our probable selves, exist now, exploring the same significances we do, expanding their meaning as we do for all of us). Counterparts, a new term in this book and so far as I know a uniquely Sethian concept, are entities existing in the same system of reality as we do, in the same time slot, but in a different space. Any groups of people exploring the same area of significance are counterparts in this sense, some more closely akin than others, whether or not they are aware of it.

To this band of "alternate selves" I would like to introduce another group: Those selves that we have been and will be in this lifetime, who exist now and are busily exploring meaning from their perspective, influencing us as we influence them. The me of age five is not the me of now; both of us exist, both exploring significance, both influencing one another, as the me of five years from now presently in existence is not "me," yet the version of me most likely, given the me of now, as I am the most likely version of her given who she is this instant. These selves, like reincarnational selves in that they exist in the same reality system but in different time slots, are for some of us the only alternate selves that we have any or much awareness of, which makes them especially useful in making sense of our present reality.

In your imagination, go wherever you need to go in order to meet all of these different versions of yourself, all of these focuses of your own consciousness. This is your consciousness in its expanded, multidimensional form, the consciousness you have come to know in dreams and in other exercises of this sort. Feel your ego consciousness extend, merge, and become one with the ego consciousness of these "other" entities; feel yourself as a consciousness containing all of these points of view at once, simultaneously having been in a multitude of theaters at once. Feel yourself owning the skills and wisdom of this conglomerate group of entities, you in all these guises, the material manifestation of your psyche. Feel all of these entities as part of you. You know how it feels to contain within you your three-year-old self and the teenager; all of the different selves you have been in your lifetime are now the conglomerate you. Extend this feeling of conglomeration to include reincarnational selves, counterparts, and probable selves; feel them reverberate as part of your being, your consciousness. Reach the Seth level of consciousness, see how it feels to have this multiple awareness.

When you come back to space-time as "you," hold the afterglow of that feeling of unity and interconnectedness, savor the feeling. Know that through summoning up that feeling you can get in touch with and support from those parts of your larger consciousness.

Exercise #91

Try this when you're in the deep country, alone—unless your digs are relatively soundproof.

Bellow, bawl, shriek and scream, kick, flail your arms, weep and wail. Put on a broad grin, giggle, chuckle, laugh—and laugh and laugh. Scowl, leer, utter imprecations. Yell insults. Curl up in a ball and shiver. Shake. Shake yourself up, jump, reach high, jump and reach and jump and reach. Slowly turn, softly stroke your arm, murmur, sit, cradle your head, hum a lullaby. Stand, salute the flag, and join the parade, march two three four, march two three four. Change to ONE two three, ONE two three, ONE two three, and waltz and spin and waltz and spin. Sink down, rest, and reflect.

Reflect on how you felt with each action, each sound you made. Reflect on how your feelings changed as your actions and sounds did. Reflect on how actions and sounds symbolize feelings, how through actions and sounds you can summon up feelings. It is not a one-way street in which you feel and then your body reacts. Your body, through its actions and sounds, elicits the "appropriate" feelings—or changes one feeling to another.

Exercise #92

Think of an ability you would like to develop in yourself. Imagine yourself in the future having developed this ability to its utmost. Really exaggerate, pull out all stops. Summon up the facial expressions, gestures, movements, and feelings and draw them out. Create a scenario in which you are using this ability, demonstrating your expertise, winning much deserved accolades. Enjoy.

Exercise #93

In this final consciousness-stretching exercise, use X-ray vision. See through walls. If you are outside, look in, if inside, look out. Know you can develop this ability. En masse we create characters like Superman to remind us of our unused abilities, to symbolize our human potential. Develop X-ray vision!

Exercise #94

Are you ready for this? Create a nightmare.

Write a waking dream that is a nightmare. You might get into the mood for it by recalling nightmares you have had, or movies that frightened you, books or stories, TV. Let yourself go and get into that horror. Gravitate toward the scariest images, feel them, let them change before your eyes. Write them down and compare your images here with dream images.

Exercise #95

List those people connected with your life in some way whom you strongly dislike. After each person, jot down the reason you dislike him or her—actions, traits, appearance.

Now in your imagination, become each person on your list. Put yourself in that person's shoes, looking out at the world from his or her eyes. Look at yourself from this person's point of view. How does this person see you?

After you have "been" each person on the list, become a composite of those people, taking on traits from each. See how it feels to be all of these people combined together, looking at you. What do they see?

Do you still dislike those people?

Exercise #96

Create a multiple waking dream for yourself—a double, triple, quadruple, quintuple, whatever-you-can-manage dream. A single dream with several threads of action going on simultaneously, all of them related by theme. Visualize an onion with its multiple layers, visualize the dream, all of a piece, but multilayered. Let it unfold itself to you.

Exercise #97

Create your own reincarnation. Imaginatively choose the parents you want, your siblings, where you'll live, when, the challenges you'll deal with, physical attributes, skills, feelings, and tone. Have a ball!

Index